Routledge Revivals

Writings on Imperialism and Internationalism

J. A. Hobson's *Imperialism: A Study*, first written in 1902, was undoubtedly his most prolific work. Yet Hobson wrote frequently about the topic of imperialism over the course of his career, and a number of his articles are included in this collection, first published in 1992. Exploring areas such as the presence of capitalism in South Africa following his visits to the country in the lead-up to the Boer War, free trade, and the ethical implications of empire, these articles and extracts reflect how Hobson's ideas changed over the decades in which they were written. This is a fascinating collection of material that provides an unparalleled depth of insight into the views of one of the most important economic thinkers of the early twentieth century.

Writings on Imperialism and Internationalism

J. A. Hobson

Routledge
Taylor & Francis Group

First published in 1992
by Routledge/Thoemmes Press

This edition first published in 2013 by Routledge
2 Park Square, Milton Park, Abingdon, Oxon, OX14 4RN

Simultaneously published in the USA and Canada
by Routledge
711 Third Avenue, New York, NY 10017

Routledge is an imprint of the Taylor & Francis Group, an informa business

© 1992 Routledge/Thoemmes Press

All rights reserved. No part of this book may be reprinted or reproduced or
utilised in any form or by any electronic, mechanical, or other means, now
known or hereafter invented, including photocopying and recording, or in any
information storage or retrieval system, without permission in writing from the
publishers.

Publisher's Note
The publisher has gone to great lengths to ensure the quality of this reprint but
points out that some imperfections in the original copies may be apparent.

Disclaimer
The publisher has made every effort to trace copyright holders and welcomes
correspondence from those they have been unable to contact.

A Library of Congress record exists under LC control number: 94131559

ISBN 13: 978-0-415-82509-2 (hbk)
ISBN 13: 978-0-203-38375-9 (ebk)
ISBN 13: 978-0-415-82542-9 (pbk)

WRITINGS ON IMPERIALISM AND INTERNATIONALISM

J.A. Hobson

Edited with an Introduction by
Peter Cain

ROUTLEDGE / THOEMMES PRESS

© 1992 Routledge / Thoemmes Press

Published in 1992 by
Routledge / Thoemmes Press
11 New Fetter Lane
London EC4P 4EE

Reprinted 2000

J.A. Hobson: A Collection of Economic Works
6 Volumes: ISBN 0 415 08304 4

The articles reprinted here were originally
published between 1891 – 1930

Routledge / Thoemmes Press is a joint imprint
of Routledge and Thoemmes Antiquarian Books Ltd.

Publisher's Note

These reprints are taken from original copies of each book. In
many cases the condition of those originals is not perfect, pages
having suffered from such things as inconsistent printing
pressures, show-through from one side of a leaf to the other,
the filling in of some letters and characters, unstable, often
handmade, paper and the break up of type. The publisher has
gone to great lengths to ensure the quality of these reprints but
points out that certain characteristics of the original copies
will, of necessity, be apparent in reprints thereof.

INTRODUCTION

There is no doubt that the book for which J. A. Hobson is best known is *Imperialism: A Study*, first written in 1902. The book went through three editions in his lifetime, the last of them in 1938 two years before his death, when Hobson wrote a new introduction but left the original text substantially unaltered (Hobson, 1988). *Imperialism* is undoubtedly Hobson's most comprehensive and impressive statement of his position. Nonetheless, in a writing life of fifty years, Hobson wrote about imperialism on many occasions and this collection of articles and extracts demonstrates that his perspectives and even his judgements on these matters changed frequently, often in direct response to crises in the political and economic world around him (Cain, 1978; 1990).

'Free Trade and Foreign Policy' (Article 2), written in 1898 in response to the battle between the great powers for spheres of interest in China, was Hobson's first attempt to offer a comprehensive theory of imperialism (Porter, 1968; Cain, 1985a). He was concerned to refute the assumption of the imperialists that extending British imperial authority abroad was vital for trade and for economic survival and he did so by denying the necessity of the link between foreign trade and growth. The root problem of the economy was a maldistribution of resources which left too little of the income of the nation in the hands of the mass of consumers and meant that a large percentage of what was annually produced and saved had to find foreign outlets. Imperialism was the military and political manifestation of under-consumption and of the search for new markets for foreign investment to relieve the crises caused thereby: its antidote was social reform, which by redistributing income and wealth more fairly, would lead to the absorption of the surplus domestically and to a drastic reduction in the need for overseas markets for capital and, therefore, for goods. All the crucial ingredients of the argument of *Imperialism: A Study* are here. What is missing, however, is the claim made in the larger work that the galvanizing force behind imperial policy was financial conspiracy. That element owed its prominence to Hobson's journalistic visits to South Africa made in the run-up to the Boer War when he became convinced that the war was being fought on behalf of the mineowners backed by a kept press. The specifics of his South African experience are not strongly evident in *Imperialism: A Study*, where the argument proceeds on a high plane of generality, but can be found in *The War in South Africa* (1900), in the article 'Capitalism and Imperialism in South Africa' (Article 3) and in later works (Article 6 and Etherington, 1984).

One of the grand themes of *Imperialism: A Study* is that the vast waves of foreign investment upon which imperialism was built would lead in time to an industrial revolution in what we now call the Third World, devastating its traditional cultures. The consequent de-industrialization of the developed world would also turn Western Europe into a service economy, ruled by financial power, destructive of the liberty and demo-cracy which Hobson associated with the rise of urban industry (Cain, 1979). The argument can be found in Part II of *Imperialism* (Hobson, 1988 pp. 285—327), but it relies upon ideas first formulated by Hobson in 'Can England Keep Her Trade?' (Article 1) written in 1891 long before he became interested in imperialism and when he was concerned more directly with the problem of poverty in Britain. Given his narrow perspective at the time, Hobson was quite willing to suggest protection and the prohibition of capital export as remedies. By 1898, of course, he was claiming that social reform would solve the problem by reducing the volume of foreign trade to relative insignificance. In *Imperialism* he also showed himself a passionate advocate of free trade, arguing that tariffs were simply a device for ensuring that the poor would pay the costs of imperial expansion. But his most explicit attack on tariffs in this context was made in his article 'The Inner Meaning of Protectionism' (Article 4), Hobson's response to Chamberlain's announcement of his campaign for imperial preference and empire unity in 1903. In this article he claimed that protection would simply add to the underlying problem of maldistribution, increasing the need for overseas outlets for trade and capital and adding to the pressure of imperial expansion. Free trade, on the other hand, since it fostered peaceful intercourse between nations, was an essential basis of pacific internationalism.

In *Imperialism*, Hobson briefly identified the South of England as an example of a service economy living off the fruits of imperialist exploitation (Hobson, 1988 pp. 151, 313—4), but his only extended analysis on these lines was made in 'The General Election: A Sociological Interpretation' (Article 7). Here, Hobson examined the deep divide, evident in the results of the January 1910 election, between the North of England, whose allegiance was to the Liberal party, and a predominantly Conservative South. Hobson believed that the electoral division reflected a fundamental cleavage between the provincial industrial sector in Britain, which under the Liberals was increasingly inclined to support an extension of democracy and social reform, and a service economy dominated by a 'moneyed class' whose income often came from overseas investments and who provided the main source of support for imperialism (Cain, 1985b).

The Liberals came to power in 1906 and retained it in 1910 in two elections. They were committed to measures of social reform such as old age pensions and compulsory insurance against sickness and unemployment which were consistent with Hobson's own ideas on the subject. Hobson had always believed, as 'The Inner Meaning of Protectionism' (4) testifies, that in the very long run the forces making for international harmony would prevail over those supportive of war and imperialism. But after 1906, he seems to have assumed that the pace of this inexorable drift towards world-wide free trade and democratic internationalism had quickened. One of the best introductions to this strain in Hobson's thought can be found in the 1906 article 'The Ethics of Internationalism' (Article 5) with its underlying idealist teleology. This brings out the extent to which he believed that, although world relationships were still disfigured by imperialism, the main effect of international trade and investment was to forge cooperative bonds between peoples and lay the basis for internationalism (Porter, 1990).

It was during this period of Liberal reformism that Hobson wrote *The Economic Interpretation of Investment* (Article 8), a work in which he offered, for a complex of reasons (Cain, 1978), an approach to imperialism seriously at variance with that put forward in *Imperialism: A Study*. In *Economic Interpretation* (8) he argued that an extensive foreign trade was in the interests of all classes of the population and that foreign investment represented merely the excess savings of the nation which would otherwise find no domestic outlet. Moreover, overseas investment was always beneficial to the receiving country which was incorporated into a harmonious system of international division of labour. His radical analysis of capitalism was now muted and all the fears about the disastrous consequences of international factor movement for the world economy which had preoccupied him earlier now disappeared. It is also apparent that Hobson now viewed imperial domination over 'backward nations' as an inevitable stage in a progress towards a new and better world.

Of course, the coming of the First World War and the international economic disarray which succeeded it, forced Hobson to recant a great deal of this (Cain, 1990). In 'Why the War Came as a Surprise' (Article 10) he acknowledged the facile nature of the optimism amongst radicals in the years just before the War and then went on to claim that imperialism based on inequalities in Europe was one of the underlying causes of discord between the Great Powers, though he was also inclined to admit that Germany bore a special responsibility for starting the conflict in 1914. But after 1914 he did not revert to the confident assumption of the late 1890s that Britain's foreign trade could largely be dispensed with in a new moral order. Indeed, in *The New Protectionism* (Article 9), written in the middle of the war, he went out of his way to persuade his readers that it was quite wrong to assume that, after the war was over, it would be good policy to exclude Germany from our markets because restoring trade between the belligerents was important in re-establishing peace on a firm basis. *The New Protectionism* (9) is also worth reading because it contains a fine example of Hobson's passionate conviction that permanent peace between the European Powers would only be possible if the economic development of colonial territories took place in future under internationally agreed rules. However, the chief interest of the book lies in the fact that, in looking back to the pre-war imperialist rivalries of the European powers in Africa and Asia, Hobson appeared to accept their aggression as unavoidable. He also admitted that, on balance, imperialism had brought considerable commercial benefits.

However, during the war, and particularly in *Democracy After the War* (Article 11), he reiterated many of the arguments of *Imperialism: A Study*, adding also his belief that rapid increases in productivity in industry just before the war had exacerbated the problem of oversaving and increased imperialist pressures. *Democracy After the War* (11) is also important because it offers analyses of a number of specific imperialist episodes, something quite rare in Hobson's work. These include the occupation of Egypt, the second Boer War and the British role in the scramble for China in the immediate pre-war period. The conclusions to which he came were fundamentally the same as in *Imperialism: A Study*, but he showed a much greater awareness of historical complexity. Significantly, the crudely conspiratorial element present in the earlier work had now disappeared and he was willing to concede that the motives of some of the powers in China, such as Japan and Russia, could not be adequately described as economic or financial.

After 1918, Hobson joined the Labour party where there was considerable sympathy with his ideas on underconsumption and, in the 1920s and 1930s when unemployment and depression overshadowed the world economy, his writings reflect these preoccupations. One important problem which concerned him was that attempts to raise living standards for the average man in Britain could fail because costs would rise and British exports would be priced out of world markets. In *Rationalisation and Unemployment* (Article 12) he recognized that overcoming this difficulty would involve cooperation between the industrial powers to raise living standards in step with each other, thus avoiding cut-throat competition abroad. A new attitude to 'backward' countries under imperialist control was also needed. Living standards in these parts of the world were very poor and imports low, placing a real restraint on the growth of trade with industrial countries like Britain. Only a concerted effort to raise incomes in the underdeveloped world, a benign imperialism, could provide Britain with the markets necessary to avoid the perils of underconsumption and unemployment. This is a far cry from the message of *Imperialism: A Study*.

In the late 1930s, for complex reasons, Hobson reverted to the views he had held at the beginning of the century and this made it possible for him to reprint *Imperialism: A Study* practically unchanged (Cain, 1990 pp. 47—9). As a result of the prestige and importance of *Imperialism* and Hobson's silence about his frequent changes of emphasis in his autobiography *Confessions of an Economic Heretic* published in 1938, a rich seam of Hobsonian reflections on imperialism were thus lost to view until now.

Peter Cain
University of Birmingham, 1992

REFERENCES

Cain, P.J. (1978) 'J.A. Hobson, Cobdenism and the Radical Theory of Economic Imperialism'. *Economic History Review*, Vol. 31!

———— (1979) 'International Trade and Economic Development in the Work of J.A. Hobson before 1914'. *History of Political Economy* Vol. 11.

———— (1985a) 'Hobson, Wilshire and the Capitalist Theory of Capitalist Imperialism'. *History of Political Economy* Vol. 17.

———— (1985b) 'J.A. Hobson, Financial Capitalism and Imperialism in Late Victorian and Edwardian England'. *Journal of Imperial and Commonwealth History* Vol. 13.

———— (1990) 'Variations on a Famous Theme: Hobson, International Trade and Imperialism' in Freeden, M. (ed.) *Reappraising J.A. Hobson: Humanism and Welfare*. London: Unwin Hyman.

Hobson, J.A. (1988) *Imperialism: A Study*. London: Unwin Hyman.

Etherington, N. (1984) *Theories of Imperialism: War, Conquest and Capital*. Beckenham: Croom Helm.

Porter, B. (1968) *Critics of Empire: British Radical Attitudes to Colonialism in Africa 1895—1914*. London: Macmillan.

———— (1990) 'Hobson and Internationalism' in Freeden, M. (ed.) *Reappraising J.A. Hobson: Humanism and Welfare*. London: Unwin Hyman.

CONTENTS

Article 1

THE
NATIONAL REVIEW.

No. 97.—MARCH, 1891.

CAN ENGLAND KEEP HER TRADE?

TWELVE years ago the manufacturers of Lancashire were agitating for the abolition of the tariff upon cotton goods imported into India. This tariff was abolished in 1880. The same manufacturers are now crying out for a Factory Act to regulate hours of labour, and to impose other restrictions upon native producers in India.

The Bombay and Calcutta mills, we are told, are reproducing all the worst iniquities which disgrace the early history of our English factory system. Nothing is more likely. But the motive which is inducing our Lancashire producers to their urgent request for legislative protection is not a spirit of disinterested philanthropy. It is a well-founded fear of Indian competition. The industrial growth of India during the last fifteen years deserves more than a passing recognition. Her imports in 1888 amounted to more than £65,000,000, nine-tenths of which were English goods. India is, in fact, the largest market which English manufacturers possess, and as Sir R. Temple significantly remarks, " next after that of China, is also the greatest they could possibly obtain in the present condition of the world." They are by far the largest purchasers of our cotton goods, hardware, and machinery, and wrought metal of every kind.

One-third of our shipping trade is with India. A great part of this enormous trade is the growth of the last fifteen years. The import of cotton goods into India rose from £18,760,000 in 1879 to £28,674,000 in 1886. The growth of exports has kept pace with the import trade, amounting in 1888 to £90,000,000. It is to the nature of this export trade, and of the general commercial development of India that our chief attention is due. The great wheat export trade of India is a thing of the last twelve years ; the quantity we now take from India is more than five times what we took ten years ago.

To the eyes of the British merchant this is entirely as it should be. India should be, for all eternity, a huge field for the growth of grain and cotton to be exported to England and paid for in manufactured goods. What arrangement can be more simple and delightful !

But how if it be not the eternal destiny of India to provide us with cheap grain and raw material of manufacture ? Why should not India manufacture for herself what she wants, and keep her grain to feed her toiling millions ? Sir John Strachey, in his recent book on India, tells us " The expansion of trade has been more rapid in India during the last ten years than in any other country of the world. Between 1873 and 1884 the foreign trade of Great Britain was stationary, and even suffered a slight diminution ; the trade of France and of Germany increased by about 7 per cent., and that of the United States by 21 per cent., while the increase was 60 per cent. in India."[*] Of this increase the growth of manufactures has been rapid and persistent. Between 1876 and 1886 the number of mills and factories in India had nearly doubled. It is estimated that the Indian cotton factories now represent a capital of more than £10,000,000. In 1876 there were only fifteen mills at work in the Bombay Presidency ; there are now seventy-two, and ten more are said to be in process of construction. An important foreign trade in manufactures has sprung up with China and other Asiatic countries. In 1876 this trade was estimated at £1,000,000 ; in ten years time it had risen to £4,200,000. It is now an admitted fact that India is supplanting England in the Asiatic market. In spite of the repeal of import duties on manufactured cotton goods, the native manu- factures have doubled within the last eight years. The exports of cotton goods from the United Kingdom to China and Hongkong showed a slight falling off in 1887, as compared with 1880, while Indian exports during the same interval had multiplied threefold. But the most significant figures are those recently published by the Board of Trade. In May 1890 no less than 12½ per cent. of Indian exports consisted of partly or wholly manufactured goods, while the same return shows an absolute decline in the imports of manufactured goods from Great Britain as compared with the previous year. A comparison of imports and exports of yarns and textile fabrics between 1889 and 1890 shows a slight diminution in imports from England and a slight growth in exports from India, which clearly indicates a turn in the balance of trade. The same tables establish the fact that while the total imports into India are almost stationary, the total exports show an expansion of 12 per cent.[†] Further evidence of the growth of native cotton

[*] *India*, by Sir J. Strachey, K.C.B.
[†] *The Board of Trade Journal*, September 1890, p. 382.

manufacture is afforded by the diminished export of raw cotton to England, which shrank from £5,884,985 in 1884 to £3,063,002 in 1888.

From these facts, and many others, it is evident that India is learning to manufacture for herself, and is already able to compete successfully with England in neighbouring Asiatic markets.

Now, the first question which suggests itself is this, How has India been enabled so lately to develop this industrial energy?

The answer is not far to seek. The whole of this commercial development is the direct product of English capital and English enterprise. We have laid more than sixteen thousand miles of railway, and nearly thirty thousand miles of telegraph; we have rendered navigable large pieces of the Ganges, Brahmaputra, and a dozen other rivers, laid metal roads, and assisted in the making of twenty thousand miles of canals; we have opened supplies of coal and iron in different parts of the country; railway plant and rolling-stock still form the most rapidly increasing form of imported manufacture. We have not merely sent over our machinery and taught natives how to use it, but we have stimulated the native manufacture of machinery to such an extent that, as we now see, the import of English machinery seems likely to be checked. In a word, it is capital owned and directed by an English Government and English private companies which is laying the solid foundations of the manufacturing future of India.

Since we already see that Bombay and Calcutta factories, manufacturing piece-goods on English models with English machinery, are able to oust us from Asiatic trade, it is not unreasonable to ask whether they may not in time be able to drive us from other markets, and eventually to take our place as the first manufacturing nation of the world. In a word, may we not be raising up a rival who will better our instruction and take our place? The fanatical Free-trader, jealous for his fetish, no doubt sniffs economic heresy in the very use of the term "rival" to express an industrial competitor. We can, he thinks, have nothing to fear but everything to gain from the commercial success of other nations. Well, this is an amiable and pleasant doctrine to hold, but let us look at it for a moment in the light of recent English history.

If we look at the internal history of England during the last century and a half, we shall see a widespread and strongly marked disturbance and re-settlement of industry attesting the operation of the forces grouped together under the name of the industrial revolution. At the close of the seventeenth century the largest cities, after London, were Bristol, Norwich, York, and Exeter, and the most thickly-populated counties after Middlesex and Surrey were Gloucestershire, Somerset, and Wilts, the manufacturing district

1 *

of the West, Northamptonshire and Worcestershire, the seat of the Midland manufacturers, and the agricultural counties of Hertfordshire and Bucks. The great commercial cities of to-day, Liverpool, Manchester, Birmingham, Leeds, and Sheffield were all of them towns with a population of a few thousands each.

So far as the balance of trade between the different districts of England is concerned, the industrial development of the last century and a half has wrought a complete revolution. The five most populous counties outside the Metropolitan area are Lancashire, Durham, Stafford, Warwick, and the West Riding. In 1700 none of these ranked amongst the first ten. It is needless to ask what the cause of this mighty change has been. Superior economy in the arts of production, due principally to an easier access to supplies of coal and iron, have brought these localities to the fore. It is free competition among the different districts of England that has led to a growing concentration of trade on those spots possessed of the greatest natural economic advantages.

Now, if the spirit of effective free competition works such potent changes within the narrow limits of our little island, depleting some districts of their industry and population in order to enrich and render populous other districts, what prodigious changes may we not expect when the same forces are operating with equal effectiveness over the wider range of the British empire, or even of the whole commercial world? May we not expect the same rapid rise and fall of the commercial importance of countries which we have seen in the counties of England. Is it absurd to suppose that England herself may sink, like Norfolk or Huntington before the power of some vast new Lancashire? Is it so grossly improbable that India might become the Lancashire of the British Empire, or even perhaps with China become the workshop of the world? The problem is essentially a new one, for the conditions of effective world-wide competition are only beginning to be realised. The new creation of steam-driven machinery, the material embodiment of the industrial revolution, has scarcely touched the huge countries of the East, and even in the West its full working has not been felt outside the narrow limits of a few leading nations.

Race, language, inherited prejudices, ignorance, timidity, inadequate communication, have furnished a formidable barrier to the free operation of commercial competition outside the limit of the nation which is being but gradually broken down.

In order to master the true meaning of the movement, we must look not at the international exchange of products, commonly known as foreign trade, but rather at the international transfer of capital and labour. It was the movement of capital and labour in search of the most advantageous field of investment which caused the new settlement of English commerce. It is to this movement that we must directly confine our attention, if we would understand the wider disturbance which the new spirit of industry is likely to create in order to effect a new world-wide settlement.

Capital always tends to attach itself to the cheapest labour to be found within its field of investment. Until quite recent times, this field of investment was in almost all cases practically confined to the country in which the capitalist lived. Except in rare instances, capital was not to be trusted outside the limit of effective personal supervision. The gradual breaking down of international barriers to trade, and the rapid facilitation of means of communication causes a constant expansion of the field of investment, both for capital and labour. The attraction of effective capital and cheap labour for one another is mutual. Thus a mutual gravitation takes place, capital goes out to cheap labour, cheap labour comes in to effective capital. At first capital is heavier and less mobile: the earlier effects of growing international communication is to draw cheap labour to the vicinity of capital; slave-stealing and slave-breeding, free importation of cheap foreign labour, are the natural results of the early operation of free competition outside the nation. But this movement will not and cannot last.

The following forces act as growing checks on the movement of cheap labour to the vicinity of capital:

1. The tendency of democratic government in commercial countries is against it. First, the importation of slave-labour is prohibited. Next, growing restrictions are placed upon the importation of cheap foreign labour, which have their logical culmination in an alien law pressed upon a democratic government by the large class of enfranchised workers whose interests are directly affected by the competition of the immigrants. The United States and Australia are already far advanced in this policy of restriction, for the problem has come upon them with a dramatic force which forbade that it should be shirked. A few ship-loads of Chinamen emptied into the port of London, would compel the English Government to a speedy policy of similar restriction. It will become more and more difficult for cheap foreign labour to move towards capital.

2. While the international movement of labour, in spite of growing facility of migration becomes more restricted, the movement of capital continually becomes more free. Each year sees it more fluid and more cosmopolitan. Growing knowledge of the world, the spread of secure and responsible government, the power of adequate supervision conferred by the railway, the steam-

ship, the newspaper, and the telegraph, the speculative boldness of modern business, all conduce to this mobility of capital.

Every year sees a larger and larger proportion of new English capital seeking investment in foreign lands, gravitating in ever larger quantities towards the lands of cheap labour. Although no exact statistics on the subject are available, it seems likely that about £150,000,000, some 12 per cent. of the total annual income of this country, is already derived from foreign investments.

Even if no legislative restriction were placed upon the flow of cheap labour, it seems inevitable in the long run that the early current of cheap labour should dry up, and that a reverse current should set in, capital flowing to the lands of cheap labour.

The reason of this is obvious. The cheapness of labour consists in the difference between the nett produce of that labour and the cost of subsisting that labour in accordance with the standard of living in vogue among the labourers. Chinese and Indian coolies cannot live and work so cheaply in America, Australia, or England, as in their own countries. Thus, other things being equal, it will pay capital best to employ labour in that country where it can be subsisted most cheaply. At first, other things are not equal ; capital is timid and will not move, hence labour is, for a time, drawn into countries where it is subsisted less cheaply than at home. The growing venturesomeness of capital is sufficient of itself to overcome this tendency. English and American capital must in the long run find their employment in countries where life can be most cheaply supported. Indian and Chinese labour will be found, in fact, to be cheaper when occupied in India and China than elsewhere.

In a word, capital must gravitate towards the localities where life is most easily sustained. It is now, perhaps, time to deal with the objection which takes the form of the question : Is Indian labour really cheapest? Will the nett advantage of employing Eastern labour be really great enough to draw capital from employment in England? Though Indian wages may be 3d. and English wages 3s. per diem, it is conceivable that English labour, assisted by the local advantages of more effective organization and readier supply of capital, should be more than twelve times as productive as the other. This may be so, and may continue to be so. We cannot dogmatize. If English labour does continue to be twelve times as effective as Indian labour, we have nothing to fear. But curiosity will still prompt us to put the question : Are we justified in supposing that the full superiority of English labour will be maintained ?

Examining the subject in cool blood, must we not rather look forward to a time when the difference in effectiveness of English and Indian labour will be so much diminished that our English labourer will no longer be equal to twelve Hindoos, but only to two. For we must never forget that the relative effectiveness of labour at present is much more due to the advantages in organization, and communication, and easy supply of machinery and steampower than to the actual difference in quality of labour-power in the English and Indian labourer. That the Englishman, both in physical strength, acquired skill, intelligence, and *morale*, is superior to the Hindoo no one will question; but that this superiority is rightly measured by the difference in wages between 3d. and 8s. is not for one moment to be maintained. This being so, all our efforts to civilize India, to teach her the arts of industry, to develop her factory system by the application of English capital and enterprise, to economize the industrial forces of the country by improved communications, and lastly to open up the vast hidden supplies of coal and iron she possesses, will end by making Indian labour much more effective than it has been in the past.

What will be the consequence of this growing effectiveness of Indian labour? Let us assume that, by education and improved economy of organization, Indian labour can be raised to half the effectiveness of English labour, what effect will the progress have on English industry? If English wages remained at 3s. while Indian wages stood at 3d., every rise in effectiveness of Indian labour would exercise a more powerful attraction upon English capital, which would flow with ever-growing facility to the land of most profitable investment. This movement of capital would signify a diminishing demand for English labour, and an increasing demand for Indian labour. Therefore Indian wages would begin to rise and English wages to fall. As Indian labour became more and more effective, and English capital increased in mobility, this double process would go on with ever quickening pace. Assuming an absolute fluidity in capital, it would not cease until an exact equation of productive power, relative to wages, was reached; that is to say, assuming that no improvements could make Indian labour more than half as effective as English labour, the rise of Indian wages and the fall of English wages would proceed until the former rose from 3d. per diem to, say, 9d., while the latter fell from 3s. to 1s. 6d. If English labour were in fact equally fluid with English capital, it would follow every movement of the latter. Assuming the perfect indifference and adaptability of the "economic" man as he appeared in the text-books of Ricardo and his followers, every migration of English capital to a land of cheaper labour and higher profits would draw after it a corresponding migration of English labourers. Just as the economy of centralized production in Lancashire, Staffordshire, and in the large cities of England, has drained the population of neighbouring agricultural districts, so the economy of production on Indian soil would draw the labouring population from England. If labour must in the long run follow capital, and if capital naturally seeks investment in localities where life is most easily sustained, then these lands of cheapest sustenance must, in the long run, be the centres of thickest population, and form the workshop of the world. The ideal of free trade in capital and labour would map out the habitable world according to nett effectiveness of labour, and would localize capital and labour in exact proportion to the grades of effectiveness in the various localities. Thus the capacity for the production of material forms of wealth would ride roughshod over all the higher purposes of life, distributing mankind not according to the requirements of moral and intellectual advance, or even of aggregate physical well-being, but according to that method of division which was conducive to the largest nett aggregate of wealth.

This ideal, like most ideals, may never be reached, for it assumes a perfect fluidity of both capital and labour. So far as capital is concerned, we can see no limits to the increased fluidity. But labour is in the long run much less mobile. Local attachments are so strong that a very substantial gain is required to induce emigration even to localities where the conditions of life are not widely different from those of the native land. But local attachment would not be the chief barrier in such a case as we are contemplating. The deepest difference in the flexibility of capital and labour lies in the definite character of the latter. Capital is protean, it can assume any shape, and live in any climate ; labour, embodied in human shapes, is subject to limitations of climate, health, food, &c., which render its adaptation to a new local environment very slow. Though the wages in India rose to double the English standard, the migration of English labourers would be very slow. It would probably be easier to learn to live on lower wages at home than to adapt life to an Indian or Chinese environment. Thus the rapid development of Asia would, at any rate for a long time, enable Asiatic labour to gain at the expense of European labour.

But slow, though none the less sure, would be migration of labour along the line of least resistance, following the movements of capital, to the lands of cheapest subsistence. For though the fluidity of capital grows much more rapidly than the fluidity of labour, it must be recognized the' 'he decay of customary, political, and commercial restraints, . .. growth of knowledge and of facility of communication, which belong to the spirit of modern times, increase the adaptability of labour.

The "economic" man who, as capitalist, places his capital wherever it finds cheapest labour, as labourer, seeks the spot where the supply of capital is largest and that of labour smallest, is not a mere foolish myth, as modern writers sometimes tell us ; he is the business man of the future, the ideal which modern industrial conditions are seeking more and more to realise.

With these conditions we have got to reckon. It is a vita question for England. If we leave both capital and labour free to enter and leave England as they choose, we must be content to look forward to a not distant future when this capital will find its most profitable investment outside England, leaving English labour to starve, and, driven by starvation, to follow reluctantly in the track of migrating capital. If by this time the unity of the British Empire has become so vigorous a reality to us that we view the shift of trade and population from England to India or Egypt with the same indifference with which we have seen the rise of Lancashire and the decline of Huntingdonshire, we may await with philosophic complacency this working out of economic forces.

It would, however, be safer in so educating our sentiments not to confine our sympathies too closely to the limits of the British Empire, for though it has been convenient to illustrate cosmic movements in trade by a stress upon the competition of England with India, it would not do for us to assume that India, supposing her economic advantages sufficed to secure her the industrial supremacy, would be competent to hold it against the natural advantages of China or a developed Africa. In fact, there would be no guarantee that trade and population should not pass from the British Empire, as we know it now, to lands which lie undeveloped in their natural industrial resources. This economic aspect of the world's history is, of course, no new one. The desire for wealth has been the direct guiding spirit in all the larger migratory movements of history. Driven by the hope of better food or larger trade, races have ever been moving in search of those lands, which relatively to the condition of known productive arts, yielded the largest nett advantages. Why, then, should we disturb ourselves? The large historic movements of race and trade have been so slow that they concern the individual little more than the still slower geologic changes which he knows are ever going on. Well, these movements have been slow in the past ; but there is every reason to expect that they will be incomparably faster in the future. The inventions of the last century have broken the continuity of all previous history, so far as the latter might throw light on the pace of modern movements. The rise and fall of nations has been slow in the past because the means of effective competition have been slow. Effective competition depends on rapidity of communication. If we would understand to what degree we may expect modern movements, whether in political, social, or commercial life, to be more rapid than former movements, we must compare the pace at which men, goods, news, and ideas can travel now with the pace at which they could travel a century ago. Bearing this in mind, it is not wholly unreasonable to expect that an industrial movement which is barely perceptible in its larger outlines to-day may, within a single generation of man, have reached a magnitude which will secure for it a leading *rôle* in history. If India is really possessed of vast industrial resources which are only beginning to be developed, far less than a generation will be required to enable it to drain English capital, with the effect which we have sketched above. If we are content that the seat of industry and of population should be thus transferred, we shall look on and drift with the rapid current of economic events. If we are not content that England should lose her trade, we shall be driven to a policy of Protection. What the nature of this policy will be should not be misunderstood. Protectionists of to-day are concerned with endeavouring to support home industries by keeping out foreign goods. Such a policy will be wholly inoperative to prevent the emigration of capital. On the contrary, applied to an old country like England, such Protection would encourage the alienation of capital. If we should be determined to defeat the tendency of trade to leave England and seek a land of cheaper subsistence, we shall be compelled to seek some means of placing a prohibitive tariff on the migration of English capital.

The practical bearing of our line of argument may be summed up as follows. The Free Trade doctrine that capital and labour left alone tend to find the most productive employment is quite correct. But this consideration provides no guarantee for the continuance of trade in any particular country, as, for example, England. It also teaches us that in order to maintain the standard of wages of labourers, it will not in the long run be sufficient to check the free immigration of cheap labour from outside. If it be deemed essential that trade should be kept in England, it will eventually become necessary to pass not merely an Alien Law which might be operative as an early palliative, but to establish a policy of prohibitive taxation on exported capital, that is to say, on foreign investments.

The greatest of modern explorers is capital; it passes into the remotest corners of the world, tapping the earth at every point for minerals, testing its fertility and varied capacities of growth, gauging the strength, skill, and adaptability of the inhabitants.

In proportion as the relative industrial advantages of different localities are more widely and exactly known, capital will settle down and occupy itself exclusively on those localities where the nett economic advantages are greatest. Unless England possesses special advantages of soil, climate, position, or race which enable her to play the same part in the free competition of the whole world as she has hitherto played in the restricted competition of a few advanced nationalities occupying the best known bits of earth, she has nothing to hope for in the future of commerce. Her success in the past furnishes absolutely no guarantee for the future. It is, in fact, *primâ facie*, improbable that the free world-wide explorations of capital will leave England in her place of vantage.

If it be not India, it will be some other land of rich soil and easy subsistence which will drain our capital and trade. Should we decline to protect our country against the alienation of capital, and, preferring to let trade take its course, move along with it, another century may see England the retreat for the old age of a small aristocracy of millionaires, who will have made their money where labour was cheapest, and return to spend it where life is pleasantest. No productive work will be possible in England, but such labour as is required for personal service will be procurable. at a cheap rate, owing to the reluctance of labour to keep pace with the migration of capital. Thus, without any wild stretch of imagination, we may look forward to a revived feudalism, in which the industrial baron will rule with that absolute sway which wealth must exercise over poverty, the more sentimental or less adventurous menials who shall cling to their old country in preference to following into India, China, or Heaven knows where, the march of emr ipated capital.

JOHN A. HOBSON.

Article 2

FREE TRADE AND FOREIGN POLICY.

THE economic significance of our recent foreign policy has not
received the close attention it deserves. Posing as champions
of "open markets," we appear to be maintaining the principles and
practice of Free Trade. It is true that the very Government which
engages in this Free Trade crusade has, during its three years of
office, regulated its domestic policy by a series of financial and legislative acts of "protection" directed to secure the interests of special
social and commercial classes. These petty domestic infidelities
might well awake suspicion of the foreign policy of a party which has
never welcomed Free Trade principles in head or heart. Nevertheless,
we find the majority both of leaders and followers in the Liberal
party endorsing and supporting, apparently without qualm or hesitancy,
a working scheme of foreign policy which is in effect nothing else
than a direct repudiation both of the logic and the utility of Free
Trade.

The "Free Trade" pretensions of the open markets policy will not
bear the slightest scrutiny. The working principle it avowedly
involves is the supposition that England must be prepared to "fight
for markets," not only for the retention of our colonial possessions,
but for new markets and for the acquisition of fresh territory, or, at
any rate, for the exercise of such influence over weaker foreign
nations as shall prevent them from giving to other nations trading
advantages denied to us. This is mis-named the policy of "the open
door." In truth, it is the policy of forcing doors open and forcibly
keeping them open. Now, this use of the instruments of force in
order to win foreign trade is a violation of the primary principles of
Free Trade, and if the Liberal party consent to or condone it, they
abrogate all rightful claim to be Free Traders.

The larger meaning of Free Trade ranks it as a phase of social evolution by which, on the one hand, militarism is displaced by industrialism, and, on the other hand, political limits of nationalism yield place to an effective internationalism based upon identity of commercial interests.

To organise the forces of political nationalism in order to secure by an appeal to military power the maximum quantity of commerce for the members of a nation is, in terms of the case, to revert from a higher to a lower stage of social life. But such reversion, it may seem to some, is necessary : the appeal to the intelligent self-interest of nations has failed, or they have been compelled to sacrifice their purely industrial interests to other political considerations. If this be so, let us abandon our Free Trade pretensions, and set ourselves to the mortal struggle for markets which we are told is necessary. But let us not pretend that we are fighting the battle of Free Trade. A "freedom" initiated and maintained by military power is at best a doubtful and unstable sort of freedom. But, granting that we are justified (whatever that word may mean in international affairs) in planting both our feet in front of "the door" of the Yang-tse valley to keep it against Russia or Germany, can we seriously conceive that such "open markets," girt with garrisons and gunboats, embody the great principle which animated Cobden and the prophets of the middle century in their heroic struggle?

Cobden was a plain practical man, but he had his vision, and it was not so idle as it seems to our Liberals of to-day.

"Do you suppose," said Cobden in 1850, "that I advocated Free Trade merely because it would give us a little more occupation in this or that pursuit ? No ; I believed Free Trade would have the tendency to unite mankind in the bonds of peace, and it was that, more than any pecuniary consideration, which sustained and actuated me, as my friends know, in that struggle. And it is because I want to see Free Trade, in its noblest and most humane aspect, have full scope in this world, that I wish to absolve myself from all responsibility for the miseries caused by violence and aggression, and too often perpetrated under the plea of benefiting trade. I may say, when I hear those who advocate warlike establishments or large armaments for the purpose of encouraging our trade in distant parts of the world, that I have no sympathy with them. We have nothing to hope from measures of violence in aid of the promotion of commerce with other nations."

Addressing the Manchester Chamber of Commerce in 1862, he thus concisely summarised his teaching : "In applying Free Trade, we have renounced the principle of force and coercion."

It is quite true that a large section of the most active members of the Anti-Corn Law League, wealthy manufacturers and merchants, whose short-sighted and cold-hearted ambitions were satisfied by the victory in our domestic policy which enabled them to import cheaply raw materials and pay low rates of wages, deserted Cobden and Bright so soon as they attempted a wider application of the Free Trade doctrine.

But was Cobden right or wrong in his interpretation of the Free Trade economy? Let us calmly examine his position in the light of the more developed issues of to-day. Cobden was not a peace-at-any-price man, nor was he a Little Englander, but he believed that trade could be more safely and profitably advanced by peaceful appeals to the interests of nations than by force or threats. It is worth while to discover why this policy of Cobden has been overridden.

Three deeply rooted assumptions underlie the persistent refusal of all British Governments to apply the Free Trade principles to our foreign policy. These assumptions may be thus expressed : (1) England requires continual expansion of foreign trade ; (2) this expansion can only be adequately secured by increased armaments and an extension of the area of empire ; (3) it is sound "economy" to undergo these risks and these expenses in order to promote foreign trade.

In testing the validity of these assumptions we may conveniently postpone the first till we have examined the two latter.

Assuming, then, that a continual expansion of foreign trade is essential to England's prosperity, must we be prepared to fight for empire or for "open markets"? Is coercion the only method by which a Free Trade nation can get foreign trade? In face of an apparent unanimity of conviction that force must stand behind diplomacy in pushing trade, it would be rash to answer these questions with an abrupt dogmatic negative. But we may observe how this assumption utterly ignores the accepted theory of international trade, by reverting to a notion of commercial competition which implies an absolute antagonism of interest among competitors. Take the case of China, which is most in evidence. The necessity of obtaining and defending by force a separate sphere of British influence there is avowedly based on the belief that China represents, at any given time, a certain quantity of foreign trade, and that if Russia gets so much, Germany so much, and France so much, none will be left for England. Now, if the theory of Free Trade is sound, the notion is quite unwarranted. Even if the whole of China were thus parcelled out to other industrial nations, and these nations imposed such conditions as prohibited all direct import and export trade between England and Chinese ports—the most extreme assumption of a hostile attitude—it by no means follows that England would not reap enormous benefits in the expansion of her foreign trade. Even under the comparatively simple conditions of international trade last century the policy of directing trade policy by a mere computation of the balance of trade with each several foreign nation was detected and discarded. The suggestion that England can only secure commercial advantages from the opening up of China, by securing for herself a proper share of direct trade with Chinese ports, is virtually a return to the old fallacy, with far less excuse than had the statesmen of the eighteenth century. The most feeble recognition of the intricacies of modern trade should make us aware that an increased trade with Russia, Germany, and France, or with other nations in intimate commercial intercourse with these, arising from the monopolies of Chinese trade which they enjoyed, might ultimately prove as beneficial to our foreign trade as any expansion of direct trade with China. The protective policy of these European nations, while it undoubtedly involves a net waste of industrial energy, does not enable them to keep to themselves either the whole, or any fixed proportion, of the gains of a large new market. An international trade is, in spite of tariffs and monopolies, a method of international co-operation which assigns to all the co-operating members some share of every trade advantage which each one gains : though each may doubtless be conceived as desiring to keep the whole gain to himself, he cannot do so, but must hand over some of it to every other nation which is directly or indirectly a customer. The assignment, therefore, of spheres of influence in China or in Africa, which France, Germany, or Russia may seek to monopolise for purposes of trade, does not imply, as is apparently supposed by Liberals and Conservatives alike, a corresponding loss of markets to England. It is indisputably true that the direct trading gain will be greatest for the country which enjoys the monopoly, but the belief that all the gain can be retained by her is utterly unwarranted. It is not difficult to conceive cases where another nation might enjoy even a larger share of the results of trade than the nation which owned the private markets of this trade. For instance, if Russia and France, drawing supplies of food or raw materials of manufacture from the private estates so jealously protected by them in China, found England their best customer for these goods, we might, by making them compete with one another, suck out of them the bulk of the gain of their monopoly of market. In certain trades this is not unlikely to happen.

This is the Free Trade theory which the great majority of the members of the Liberal party in this country still profess. It furnishes a peaceable policy of expansive foreign trade. Why is it virtually ignored, or even repudiated, by the action of Liberal leaders and by the rank and file of the party ? If other nations, seized by a lust for empire and inspired by narrow conceptions of their trading interests, insist upon obtaining exclusive ownership of foreign markets by a ruinously expensive parade of force, we are not compelled to follow their example, unless we have rejected utterly the counsels of the Free Trade thinkers. We can wait and obtain cheaply, peaceably, and indirectly, our full share of the commercial benefits of these adventurous and expensive projects.

If it be urged that these indirect gains are merely hypothetical, we may reply that England is in a far stronger position than any other nation to practise this peaceful policy of abstinence, because she possesses in her shipping industry a most effective guarantee that she will obtain an adequate share in the net gains of opening up new markets. Though no complete statistics are available, measuring the quantity of the carrying trade for foreign nations which England undertakes, it is known that a very large proportion of the trade, not only between England and foreign countries, but also between foreign countries trading with each other, is carried by English ships. So long as this continues to be true, England must participate in a direct and a most important manner in every opening up of foreign markets achieved by our European trade competitors.

The assumption that England can only expand her foreign trade by extension of her Empire and her commercial spheres of influence, is thus shown to be wholly inconsistent with the theory of international trade. Expanding foreign markets may be won by peace. But it may seem that this does not dispose of the case for a "spirited" commercial policy. We cannot, it is alleged, afford to wait for the chance of indirect benefits, a pushful policy pays better. Indeed, we are bound to assume that most persons are convinced that it is "sound economy" for England to support the cost of increasing armaments and to contend with other nations for increase of her Empire and for direct participation in new markets. We need investments for British capital, outlets for our superfluous labour and enterprise, markets with "inferior" races for the disposal of our increasing manufactures. Such a policy admittedly involves risk and expense; but we possess the ships, the men, and the money, and the policy "pays."

A complete refutation of this alleged "economy" is, in the nature of the case, impossible. The full cost of a policy which visibly embroils us in "envy, hatred, malice, and all uncharitableness" towards other nations has no fixed reckoning day. To some of us it seems likely to cost in the long run all we are worth in blood, treasure, trade, and in national character. But there are certain present measurable facts, which are commonly ignored, and which yet serve to suggest that our pushful policy and our distrust of Free Trade may not, even from a short focus of expediency, be the "good business" that it seems.

Is increase of empire attended by a corresponding increase of Imperial trade? Is our increased expenditure on armaments, which is designed to support our policy of obtaining and defending new markets, justified by increase of foreign and colonial trade? These at least are questions to which some definite quantitative answer may be given.

Even those who are reluctant to measure the "greatness" of England by the number of square miles contained within the Empire, or by magnitude of population, and who dislike the risk and the expense of a spirited foreign policy, believe that we have derived some considerable and demonstrable gains of a commercial character from the pursuit of such a policy. Trade tends to follow the flag, it is maintained, and although as "Free Traders" we bring no pressure upon our colonies and protectorates to trade with us, they naturally tend to do so. Now, there is no adequate foundation for this belief, as the following table of comparison between our foreign and colonial trade during the last forty years will serve to indicate:

	IMPORTS FROM		EXPORTS OF BRITISH PRODUCE TO	
Annual Averages.	PERCENTAGE OF TOTAL VALUES.			
	Foreign Countries.	British Possessions.	Foreign Countries.	British Possessions.
1855–9	76·5	23·5	68·5	31·5
1860–4	71·2	28·8	66·6	33·4
1865–9	76·0	24·0	72·4	27·6
1870–4	78·0	22·0	74·4	25·6
1875–9	77·9	22·1	66·9	33·1
1680–4	76·5	23·5	65·5	34·5
1885–9	77·1	22·9	65·0	35·0
1890–4	77·1	22·9	67·6	34·4
1895–7	78·4	21·6	70·1	29·9

Taking the whole term of years covered by this table, we perceive that no tendency whatever is exhibited for our trade with our own possessions to gain upon our trade with foreign countries. On the contrary, both in our import and our export trade foreign countries occupy a more important relative position at the close than at the beginning of this period, and, though considerable fluctuations are visible, the general tendency in import trade, and to a less extent in export trade, is to reduce the relative importance of colonial trade.

The fact that our pushful policy throughout the world is not sensibly increasing the actual value of our trade with our possessions is made manifest by the following comparison of the years 1875, 1885, 1895, which are in no degree abnormal years:

	1875.	1885.	1895.
	£.	£.	£.
Imports from Colonies .	84,423,000 ...	84,401,000 ...	95,530,000
Exports to Colonies . .	76,655,000 ...	85,424,000 ...	76,072,000
Total . . .	161,078,000 ...	169,825,000 ...	171,602,000

While due consideration of the fall of general prices during the last twenty years enables us to read into these figures proof of substantial progress in volume of trade, it cannot be admitted that our colonial trade has justified the conviction that "trade follows the flag," and that it is therefore a profitable policy for England to plant her flag upon new tracts of territory throughout the world. For we must remember that during the last forty years, and particularly since 1884, we have added enormous tracts of territory to our possessions, removing the trade which formerly adhered to them from the category of foreign to that of colonial trade. If an increasing proportion of the globe, with an increasing proportion of its population, has been passing from foreign into British possession, while our total trade with our colonies is failing to make a proportionate advance, it is evident that commercial facts are wholly at variance with the belief that "trade follows the flag."

The following figures make this failure manifest:

	EMPIRE.		TRADE.	
Years.	Population (millions).	Area (millions of miles).	Exports and Imports of United Kingdom in million £.	Trade with British Possessions in million £.
1883	305	7 0	733	189
1884	—	—	685	183
1885	—	—	642	170
1886	—	—	618	164
1887	307	—	643	166
1888	—	—	686	179
1889	327	—	743	188
1890	—	9·2	748	191
1891	368	—	744	193
1892	—	11·0	715	179
1893	384	—	681	170
1894	—	—	682	172
1895	—	—·	702	172
1896	433	11·3	738	184

The enormous accessions of territory and population since 1884—comprising the Niger Coast Protectorate, Somali Coast Protectorate, Socotra, Pahang and other Straits Settlements, parts of New Guinea,

Bechuanaland, Zululand, Royal Niger Company's territory, British East Africa, the British South Africa Company's territory, Zanzibar and Pemba, Upper Burmah and Shan States—have been followed by no increase of colonial trade reckoned in money values, and by an increase reckoned in goods, which is not commensurate with the increase of British area and population. Little more than a quarter of our foreign trade is with our possessions, almost three-quarters is with the foreign nations to whom we have been preaching Free Trade with our lips, while we have been proving our distrust of its industrial efficacy by laying violent hands upon all the parts of the earth which appear likely to afford us markets.

In order to show the folly of offending our best customers by an irritating policy which does not even pay, in the narrowest sense, I may be allowed to quote the following figures illustrative of the growth of value of our trade with our possessions, as compared with our trade with the nations we are often invited to regard as enemies:

TOTAL TRADE WITH	1875. £.		1885. £.		1895. £.
United States . . .	94,652,000	...	117,573,000	...	130,616,000
France	74,012,000	...	58,730,000	...	67,794,000
Germany . . .	55,958,000	...	50,128,000	...	59,729,000
Russia . . .	32,055,000	...	23,932,000	...	35,424,000
	256,677,000	...	250,363,000	...	293,563,000
British Colonies .	161,078,000	...	169,825,000	...	171,602,000

From this table it appears that, not merely is the value of our trade with our most powerful competitors in empire and in commerce much larger than the total value of our trade with all our colonies, but that the growth of the former trade is considerably faster than that of the latter. With France alone our trade shows smaller in 1895 than in 1875, and even there the drop was in the earlier decennium, for a considerable advance has taken place between 1885 and 1895. Moreover, after the United States, France and Germany are by far our largest customers, and Holland is the only other nation which does a larger trade with us than Russia.

Not merely is it untrue that "trade follows the flag," and that colonial expansion is necessary in order to provide markets for our produce, but it appears that our trade with our rivals—the United States, France, Germany, and Russia—has been growing at a rate somewhat faster than the total growth of our foreign and colonial trade. and considerably faster than the colonial trade taken by itself.

It is, then, for the sake of encouraging a class of trade which is both absolutely smaller than our trade with foreign countries and which shows a smaller rate of increase (in spite of the increased area of our colonial possessions) that we are invited to expend large sums upon armaments, and to use them for the sake of territorial expansion. Is this good business?

The true " economy " of our industrial foreign policy, however, requires us to take into consideration the whole national expenditure upon armaments. The taxation imposed upon the British nation in order to support the cost of our increasing army and navy is defended chiefly on the ground that it is necessary in order to safeguard our colonial possessions and to enable us to secure new markets by increasing the area of the Empire. When Cobden and Peel fought against this policy, denouncing the increased expenditure on armaments in the " fifties," they were compelled to rely upon general considerations of prudence and economy. The folly of pressing the people with taxation during a time of peace, of increasing the insurance fund when a pacific Free Trade policy was diminishing the risks against which provision must be made, the insidious danger of allowing military authorities to direct our foreign policy and to call upon the nation blindly to defray the expenses of this policy—such was the line of argument urged in 1850.

The words uttered by Sir Robert Peel in the House of Commons, March 12, 1850, are fraught with deep prophetic significance.

" I will say, that in time of peace, you must, if you intend to retrench, incur some risks. If in time of peace you must have all the garrisons of our colonial possessions in a state of complete efficiency—if you must have all our fortifications kept in a state of perfect repair—I venture to say that no amount of annual expenditure will be sufficient ; and if you adopted the opinions of military men, who say that they would throw upon you the whole responsibility in the event of a war breaking out, and some of our valuable possessions being lost, you would overwhelm this country with taxes in time of peace."

Nothing but the unparalleled and unpredicable commercial prosperity of England, during the last fifty years, has prevented us from feeling yet the " overwhelming " pressure of the policy which Peel condemned. But while Peel saw clearly, and Cobden stubbornly maintained, the danger of basing our national policy upon the false paradox *Bellum para, si pacem velis*, the economic fallacy of this military policy was far less demonstrable than it is now. Our foreign and colonial trade in 1848, when Cobden first attacked the policy of increased expenditure on armaments, was less than £170,000,000 in value, and during the next twenty years it more than tripled in its value. If then we were warranted in taking a narrow " business " view of expenditure on armaments, it might well appear that, in view of this enormous expansion of trade, the increase of the " insurance " premium was amply justified ; or, regarding the army and navy as instruments for pushing British commerce throughout the world, we might consider their use to be attended by success.

But during the last twenty-five years this argument of " payment by results " cannot for one moment be maintained. The enormous increase of expenditure on armaments which has taken place since the beginning of the " seventies " is attended by no corresponding increase of our total trade, and, as we have already seen, the colonial trade, which might seem to offer some " business " justification of expenditure on armaments, exhibits but a trifling increase.

	Expenditure on Armaments.				Trade.
	£.				£.
1873	24,065,876	...	...	...	682,292,127
1883	29,373,867	...	...	...	732,328,649
1893	33,265,683	...	...	...	681,130,677
1897	41,238,802	...	...	...	745,422,363

It is difficult for a business man to escape the interpretation put by Mr. A. J. Wilson upon these facts.

" If the 'insurance premium' on our commerce abroad represented by the cost of our navy has risen 100 per cent. in twenty-five years, while the value of that commerce, import and export together, has not risen 15 per cent., what inference can be drawn except either that the outlay is a gross and cruel imposition upon the country, or that our conduct towards foreign nations has become so exasperating of late years as to have enormously increased the risk of war with powerful enemies, either alone or in combination against us ? "

So far as trade statistics have any value, they convict us of conducting our national trade with a reckless folly which would quickly bring any individual merchant into the Bankruptcy Court. In total contravention of our theory that trade rests upon a basis of mutual advantage to the parties that engage in it, we have undertaken enormous expenses with the object of " forcing " new markets, and we have signally failed in the attempt; the only regular and palpable result of the expenditure has been to keep us continually embroiled with those very nations who are our best customers, and with whom, in spite of all impediments of ill feeling and jealousy, our trade makes the most satisfactory advance.

One implication of our policy remains for brief consideration—the assumption that our national prosperity demands a constant expansion of external markets. This assumption is without foundation. Some considerable foreign and colonial trade we certainly require, in order to enable us to get the food and raw material we cannot produce at home : such import trade we require, and an export trade which shall correspond to it. A progressive nation, evolving new material wants, and with an increasing population, must increase her foreign trade, unless she can substitute home products for imported goods. It is, however, a grave error to regard increase of foreign or colonial trade as an index of the real prosperity of a nation. Increased trade is, indeed, a sound measure of prosperity, for it implies that an increased quantity of commodities is made and consumed; but there is no advantage in an increase of foreign, as distinct from home, trade. On the contrary, home trade is a more solid and substantial basis of industrial prosperity than foreign trade for two reasons. First, it is less amenable to fluctuations arising from commercial and pólitical policies over which we can exercise no control, and which sometimes are designed expressly for our injury. Secondly, the gain arising from home trade is double instead of single, the full advantage which both parties obtain from exchange being kept within the nation.

It is no idle platitude to urge that less attention should be devoted in our public policy to measures for acquiring foreign markets and for promoting foreign trade, and more to the development of home markets. We are not compelled to spend all our energy and super-fluous cash in wrangling with other nations for markets in Africa and Asia which will take our low-class manufactured wares.

A large majority of the working class population of Great Britain is not adequately provided with the material requisites of a decent human life. Among our own people there lies an immense potential market for the conveniences and comforts of life. A progressive nation, with an infinite capacity of developing new tastes and new needs, should harbour no fear of failing markets. Even when our popula-tion is amply provided with the clothing, hardware, and other manu-factured goods which we are forcing at so great expense upon the "lower races," a consummation which is yet remote, there is no reason why our productive energy, diverted into other channels, should not continue to find, in the ever-rising standard of national comfort, a market whose expansion is able to keep pace with every growth of industrial power. With each increase of production is created a cor-responding power of consumption vested in the owners of productive factors. If these owners of consuming power exercise it in such way as to make the standard of national consumption rise with every increase of producing power, no such pressure of the needs for foreign markets as we now experience would be felt. Why, then, it may be asked, does this pressure actually occur? Why does not an expansion of home markets take off, by a rising standard of national consumption, every increase of production? In economic terms, the answer must be this. Though a potential market exists within the United Kingdom for all the "goods" that are produced by the nation, there is not an "effective" demand, because those who have the power to demand commodities for consumption have not the desire, since their material needs are amply satisfied, while those who have the desire have not the power. Stated otherwise, the working classes of this country possess an insufficient proportion of "effective demand"; the actual rise in their standard of comfort, though in some cases considerable, has not been at all commensurate with the growth of productive power of the nation, especially in manufactures. The upper and a large section of the middle classes, who own an excessive proportion of goods that are produced, do not desire themselves to purchase and consume, and, since they cannot find a sufficient home market among the workers, are compelled to struggle with classes of other nations in the same predicament for foreign markets, which seem to them limited in extent at any given time. If direct testimony to this fact and its consequences is desired, it is found in the large surplus of our national income which, being needed neither for home consumption nor for capital in home industries, seeks foreign investments, —a sum which, though it admits no precise computation, must far exceed a total of two thousand million pounds sterling. It is possible, indeed, that the growing pressure of the need for foreign investments must be regarded as the most potent and direct influence in our foreign policy. Our surplus products, which the working classes cannot buy and the wealthier classes do not wish to buy, must find customers among foreign nations, and, since those who sell them do not even desire to consume their equivalent in existing foreign goods, they must lie in foreign countries as loans or other permanent investments. A portion of the yield of these investments is represented in the excess of our import over export values, but only a portion, a large part going to swell the sum of the investments. Thus, in the first resort, it is the excessive purchasing power of the well-to-do classes which, by requiring foreign investments, forces the opening up of foreign markets, and uses the public purse for the purposes of private profit-making.

Excepting for the legitimate purpose of furnishing such foods and raw materials as cannot be economically raised at home, the prosperity of an industrial nation does not require a constant expansion of foreign markets. A juster and more equal distribution of wealth will, by stimulating home consumption to keep pace with every increase of producing power, make our industries largely independent of the need of finding new markets in parts of the world where we stir national animosities involving incalculable risks and an expensive policy of insurance and aggression.

So long as the mass of our population remains poor, and with a slowly rising standard of comfort, while our productive power advances rapidly, the demand for a continual expansion of foreign markets is inevitable ; and since we have lost all belief in the pacific economy of Free Trade, we must continue to fight for them, if, as seems probable, we cannot get enough of them without fighting. If, however, by organisation, or by legislation, or by the concession of the employing classes to the demands of humanity and sound politics, the working classes could obtain a larger proportion of the power of " effective demand " into their hands, which they would use for the rapid raising of their standard of life, the economic and moral dangers of our present industrial foreign policy would be sensibly diminished. The struggle for foreign markets, which necessitates vast armaments, does not arise from the normal exchange of commodities between nations, but is the result of an unnatural and impolitic contraction of home markets in the advanced industrial nations of the world. Just in proportion as the proletariat of these nations obtains fuller opportunities for the satisfaction of its growing needs in a civilised progressive society, absorbing in its consumption the greater share of every increase of industrial wealth, will this insane and immoral strife for distant markets tend to disappear.

The issue, in a word, is between external expansion of markets and of territory on the one hand, and internal social and industrial reforms upon the other ; between a militant imperialism animated by the lust for quantitative growth as a means by which the governing and possessing classes may retain their monopoly of political power and industrial supremacy, and a peaceful democracy engaged upon the development of its national resources in order to secure for all its members the conditions of improved comfort, security, and leisure essential for a worthy national life.

This is no rhetorical antithesis, but the plain and very practical issue which Cobden and his friends strove to place before the Liberal party half a century ago. The refusal to face this issue, the adoption instead of a half-hearted and inconsistent Free Trade policy, has crippled the principles and grievously impaired the working efficiency of Liberalism. Recent history, forcing the economic aspects of foreign policy everywhere to the front, presents with ever stronger emphasis this choice of national life. Enlightened by the growing testimony of two generations of experience to the dangers, the expense, and the impolicy of seeking markets by forcible expansion of the area of Empire, will not the Liberal party learn at length to give to Free Trade that fuller trust which its principles demand, and the refusal of which has hitherto so grievously impaired its benefits ?

We have examined the fundamental assumptions of our present policy, and have found them utterly untenable. The prosperity of England does not depend upon continual expansion of foreign trade. Even if a constant supply of new foreign markets were necessary, they are not in fact secured by " forcing doors open " and extending the area of empire. Considered as a business expenditure for the benefit of British commerce, the cost of armaments and other measures for the forcible insurance or acquisition of commerce is shown to be a false economy.

Even now it is surely not too late to abandon the notion that we must fight for markets, and to adopt as a sounder basis of our Imperial polity the principle laid down so long ago as 1820 by a staid commission of sober-minded Englishmen, that " Commerce must be a source of reciprocal amity between nations, and an interchange of productions to promote the industry, the wealth, and the happiness of mankind."

J. A. HOBSON.

Article 3

CAPITALISM AND IMPERIALISM IN SOUTH AFRICA.

THE full significance of this evil business in South Africa is only understood when it is recognised as a most dramatic instance of the play of modern forces which are world-wide in their scope and revolutionary in their operations. Those who see one set of problems in Egypt, another in China, a third in South America, a fourth in South Africa, or trace their connection merely through the old political relations between nations, will be subjected to a rough awakening as their calculations, based on this old Separatist view, are everywhere upset. Without seeking to ignore or to disparage the special factors, physical, economic, and political, which rightly assign a certain particularity to each case, I would insist upon the supreme importance of recognising the dominance everywhere exercised by the new confederacy and interplay of two sets of force, conveniently designated by the titles International Capitalism and Imperialism. Vague as these titles are, they will serve as beginnings of our diagnosis.

The growing tendency of members of modern civilised communities to stake large portions of their property in foreign lands runs counter to all past traditions of nationalism, and sets up an antagonism between the political and the economic structure of the modern world. So long as the intercourse between nations was wholly or chiefly confined to trade or exchange of commodities, nationalism could still express the economic as well as the political status of the citizen. But the large establishment by members and classes belonging to one nation of permanent investments of capital in another country is a patent breach of the old order, destroying the very roots of the old national sentiments. For where the treasure is, there is the heart also. There are two policies open to a nation whose citizens place their economic interests outside the political limits of their country. One is to maintain a rigorous distinction between the political status and the economic interests of these citizens, to tell them plainly that all foreign investments made for the sake of private profit must be at the risk of the investor, and that under no circumstances will the State interfere to save the individual from dangers which he must be presumed to have discounted in the very terms of his investment. The other policy seeks constantly to achieve a new harmony of the political and economic interests by a continual expansion of the political area, so as to cover the new areas of economic interest established by its individual members. Neither of these courses has been clearly adopted or consistently pursued by any great nation; in fact, the refusal to accept and apply either principle lies at the root of the opportunism of all foreign politics. The former policy, indeed, which absolutely refused to use the power of the State to assist individual members in those business enter-prises for private profit which it had never sanctioned, would be a sound logical position for any nation. But it has never been adopted. In most cases, investments of British capital in foreign parts are accompanied by a certain investment of British lives, either of traders or of labourers, and where a specifically British area of invest-ment has been formed, a population of British subjects is often placed upon it. This involves a real or specious identity of interests between British capital and British lives, and the owners of the former have often secured the protection of the British State by screening themselves behind the more consistently admitted rights of British subjects to personal protection against dangers and grievances incurred in foreign countries. The limits of these rights have never been determined; but the right of missionaries, traders, explorers, and other private persons, to run any risks they like and then to call upon the British Government to save or avenge their persons has been tacitly adopted as a general practice.

The policy which definitely aims at expanding the British Empire so as to cover all new areas of British economic interest cannot, of course, be consistently pursued. For the strongest forms of inter-national capitalism consist of investments in powerful civilised states with which no interference upon such grounds 'is possible. The property and investments held by British subjects in the United States, in France or in Germany, though they are economic forces making towards a true informal political internationalism, cannot be regarded as making for political fusion of the countries.

It is in the case of small, decadent, or new countries, that alien investments exercise a dominant power in foreign policy. Turkey,

Egypt, China, the South American States, and, lastly, South Africa are prominent instances of this domination. Among these South Africa is by far the clearest and most convincing example. The phenomenally rapid rise, the peculiar nature and the narrowly restricted area of capitalist-industry in South Africa account for this.

Gold and diamonds, two commodities of small intrinsic utility and of highly-concentrated market value, "keep" South Africa. The diamond mines of Kimberley, rapidly developing from 1869 towards a now fixed output of about £4,000,000 per annum, and the gold mines of Witwatersrand, discovered only thirteen years ago, and already yielding at the rate of about £20,000,000 per annum, occupy a place of supreme economic importance in a country feebly developed in agriculture and in other industries, and sparsely peopled with some three-quarters of a million white inhabitants. If the gold and diamonds had been widely dispersed in their area, and had been workable by the old order of individual diggings or small labouring enterprise, the different structure of such industry would have had entirely different political implications. But, after a short period of open competition and small individual digging, the diamond mining crystallised into the rigid and well-nigh absolute monopoly of the De Beers Company, which has enabled Messrs. Rhodes, Beit, Barnato, Rothschild and a small handful of fellow capitalists to wield an absolute control both of the industry and the market, regulating the demand for and the price of labour, the quantity and the price of diamonds, in accordance with their calculations of a maximum profit for the company.

More important still, this same group of men with a small number of confederates, chiefly foreign Jews, representing the most highly organised form of international finance yet attained, controls the entire gold industry of the Transvaal. The names of the chief directors of the leading companies, Wernher, Beit, Eckstein, Rhodes, Rudd, Neumann, Rothschild, Albu, Goetz, Rouliot, Farrar, Barnato, Robinson, fairly indicates the distinctively international character of this financial power, as well as the closely concentrated form which it has taken. During the thirteen years that have elapsed since the definite discovery of the Rand gold fields, the concentrative forces distinctive of modern capitalism have been operating rapidly; the number of independent firms has been diminishing, and even when the independent structure of a mining business is still preserved, the cross-ownership of capital by members of other leading firms reduces the real economic independence. Moreover, since the year 1891, which may be said to have determined the future development of gold mining in the Transvaal, by the discovery of the profitable future of deep-level mining, the concentration of control has been more rapid and more certain. The Chamber of Mines, whose active life may be said to have begun in 1891, has been a chief instrument by which the " Eckstein Group," the virtual control of which rests with the men who are owners of De Beers, has fastened its supremacy upon the industry. For some time Mr. J. B. Robinson, the only strong independent figure, maintained some sort of real opposition, aided by a few French and German Companies; but during the last two years this opposition has broken down, and the dominance of Eckstein may be considered to have been secured. In the near future this power must increase, because Eckstein's has secured a well-nigh complete monopoly of the working of those deeper levels upon which the future productivity and value of the Rand depends.

Whether the net economy of working so large and complex an industry really favours an absolute amalgamation, like that of De Beers, is highly disputable. There may also be financial reasons against such a course. It must be borne in mind that in dealing with international capitalism, the forces and the interests of the investor and of the financier are by no means always identical. When we come presently to trace the political influences exerted by capitalism this becomes clearer. At present it suffices to observe that even were complete structural amalgamation of the gold mines otherwise advisable, such separation, real or apparent, as favoured the manipulation of and speculation in stocks might counteract the merely industrial economies, i.e., the shareholder might be sacrificed to the speculator. But however this may be, through the growing power of the Chamber of Mines or by direct coercion of weaker companies, it seems tolerably certain that the " Eckstein " influence will control the gold mining industry of the Transvaal. The best evidence of recent expert engineers, for example the important testimony of Mr. Curle in his work " The Gold Mines of the World," indicates that there are no other gold mines in the Transvaal, or in South Africa, except possibly a few in Rhodesia, already under the same capitalist control, which are likely to disturb the supremacy of the Rand. In all human probability, for some decades the persons who control the Rand gold mines hold the economic future of South Africa in the hollow of their hands.

Not only the rapidity and the narrow local and personal limitation of this economic dominion, but certain personal characteristics of those who wield it, deserve attention. This little group of capitalists are the real " economic men " about whom text-books of Political Economy used to prate, but who have been generally relegated to mythology. Most of them are Jews, for the Jews are *par excellence* the international financiers, and though English speaking, most of them are of Continental origin. Their interest in the Transvaal has been purely economic; they went there for money, and those who came early and made most have commonly withdrawn their persons, leaving their economic fangs in the carcase of their prey.

They fastened on the Rand, as they fastened on the Diamond Fields of Griqualand West, and as they are prepared to fasten upon any other spot upon the globe, in order to exploit it for the attainment of large profits and quick returns. Primarily they are financial speculators, taking their gains not out of the genuine fruits of industry, even the industry of others, but out of the construction, promotion and financial manipulation of companies in which a large number of smaller men are induced to put money, and out of dealing in shares of these companies. The Rand is peculiar in possessing underneath this speculative surface a sound, substantial property with a tolerably certain profitable future. The early recognition of this fact has induced this group of financial speculators to secure and retain hold of a preponderating share of this genuinely valuable property, freely selling out and buying in when markets are on the move, but never really giving up their hold upon the sources of wealth.

It is important to distinguish the interest these " capitalists " have in their holdings of such sound investments as East Rands and Ferreira Deeps, which may be described as an industrial interest seeking its reward from the profitable working of these mines, and the purely financial interest they assume in the more speculative properties which they use for Stock Exchange purposes. The difference is well illustrated by the double stake which those " capitalists " have in the present war. So far as the issue seems likely to establish security and order, and to lead to a reduction of working expenses, it profits them in their capacity of mine-owners. But independently of this, the slump last summer, followed by a quick recovery when Imperial coercion was actually secured and by the prospective " boom " when a so-called " settlement " is reached, has been and will be a separate great source of gain to these men in their capacity of stock-manipulators.

This small confederacy of international financiers, containing in their ranks a few Englishmen like Rhodes and Rudd, but chiefly foreign Jews, are the economic rulers of South Africa, for they control the mines which are the really valuable asset of the country. The *causa causans* of the present trouble in South Africa is the growing need of these economic rulers to become political rulers. These men were not by choice politicians, still less were they British Imperialists: it is only the force of extreme circumstances which drives men like Rhodes and Beit to assume their present rôle. The aversion of the true " business man " from politics is almost universal; where political barriers, tariffs or restrictive legislation block the path of profit-making, or where State aid is needed to push business or secure profitable jobs, he generally prefers to exert influence by the gentle art of bribery, rather than himself to enter the political arena. It is only when the personal exercise of legislative or administrative powers is essential to industrial prosperity that the economic man becomes politician, shedding some of his primitive cosmopolitanism and becoming loyalist and patriot.

The career of Mr. Rhodes is most instructive on this matter. During his early years in South Africa no one suspected him of harbouring those magnificent dreams of British empire which he and his friends have expounded in these later years. His entrance into political life closely coincided with the requirements of the diamond industry of Griqualand West. When that district was annexed to Cape Colony in 1880 it was very necessary that some tactful man, not too scrupulous, who well understood the needs of the diamond industry, should represent Barkly West and hold the fortress of a monopoly worth a quarter of the capitalised value of the colony. When the country passed into colonial hands there were men so audacious as to conceive the design of securing these mineral values at a fair valuation for the benefit of the colony : business men must needs enter politics to defeat such nefarious projects.

From time to time proposals have been made to tax diamonds : such proposals must be fought and vanquished. When the great amalgamation scheme of 1885 was executed, and the compound system which ruined the town of Kimberley was established, loud remonstrances were made by statesmen who well understood the dangerous power of this monopoly : the right man in the right place was required to assuage the public feeling thus aroused, and to prevent any awkward interference by the Government. Can anyone experienced in colonial life doubt that the absolute immunity from taxation which the diamond industry enjoys is due to political jobbery and intrigue? Not only is the industry untaxed ; it is not even rated for the benefit of the town of Kimberley.

Nor is that enough. The most vital principles of personal liberty are violated by the monstrous Illicit Diamond Buying law, according to which any person in the Colony may be arrested for being found in possession of an uncut diamond, and is assumed to be guilty of wrongful possession unless he can bring proof to the contrary. The "Compound" system in the Kimberley and De Beers mines, according to which a so-called voluntary labour contract is converted into a term of rigorous imprisonment with hard labour, is not merely a gross violation of the spirit of personal freedom, but is a specific establishment of that evil principle of " truck " which all progressive legislation has denounced. The large employment of convict labour in the diamond mines is another instance of the convenient alliance between politics and industrial capitalism. Is anyone bold enough to suggest that the position of special privilege and exemption enjoyed by the largest and most profitable industry of Cape Colony has been won and maintained by any other means than " by converting public trusts to very private uses ? "

I am far from believing that Mr. Rhodes has been moved exclusively or chiefly by purely financial considerations in his politics : it is quite likely that some large, indefinite desire to express his personality in what is termed " empire-building " may have fused with, and at times over-powered, the narrower financial aims. But two facts stand out clearly from his career ;—first, that he and his confederates have systematically used politics to assist their business projects ; second, that in politics they have adopted " Imperialism " as a last resort. The first public post occupied by Mr. Rhodes was that of Deputy-Commissioner in Bechuanaland in 1884-5, at the time when bodies of Transvaal Boers, presumably with the connivance of the Transvaal Government, had entered that country and established the Republics of Stellaland and Goschen. The possession of Bechuanaland by the Transvaal would have closed the road to the North against British Imperialism : this was clearly understood by the rival claimants, and when remonstrances had failed Sir Charles Warren was sent up with an Imperial force to assert the Imperial interest and to establish the Imperial control. What part did Mr. Rhodes play at this critical juncture? He threw all the weight of his influence in favour of the Transvaal and against the Imperial authority.

The following extract from a speech delivered in the Cape Assembly, and reported in the *Cape Argus*, July 16, 1884, deserves attention :

> Mr. Rhodes said :—" He proposed (last year) to the House to enter into negotiations in connection with this territory, and he warned the House that he feared the Imperial Factor would be introduced into the question before long, and with the chance of a recurrence of the unfortunate affairs which he had seen in this country . . . . The House and the country was at this moment plunged into what he foresaw— that if we did not move in the question of Bechuanaland in connection with the Transvaal Government, the Imperial Government would interfere and possibly the interference of the Imperial Government might lead to a repetition of those unfortunate occurrences which they had had in connection with the Transvaal . . . . They were running the risk of any moment of a collision with the Transvaal. It might be said that he was one of Imperial instincts, but he could ask those members of the House who were present last year to support him, for he said then that we must not have the Imperial Factor in Bechuanaland. He implored the House then to pass a resolution for acting in conjunction with the Transvaal, and he said if they did not pass it they would regret it. He said once more to them they must act . . . . They should at once negotiate with the Imperial Government and with the people of the Transvaal, and first and foremost they should remove the

Imperial Factor from the situation. He believed that if they did not, there was on the border of the Transvaal great danger for South Africa."

The comment made by Sir Charles Warren upon Mr. Rhodes' conduct runs as follows:

" There can be no doubt, to my mind, that Mr. Rhodes' action, supporting and upholding the Transvaal Party, tended to a considerable degree to prevent peace being established in Stellaland. I consider that the difficulties which occurred in Stellaland since August last were entirely of his own causing, and that had he not come into the country, Stellaland might have been in a quiet state when I arrived.

There is no reason to suppose that Mr. Rhodes was really anxious to increase the territorial power of the Transvaal, but that he feared lest the establishment of a Crown Colony or a Protectorate should interfere with his plan of a Chartered Company, under which he hoped to include Bechuanaland along with the illimitable territory of the North. As it turned out, he over-estimated both the ambitions and the powers of the Imperial factor, for ten years later British Bechuanaland was incorporated with the colony, and the Imperial control of the Protectorate was not wide awake enough to prevent Mr. Rhodes obtaining the strip of land needed for a jumping-off place in the Jameson Raid. The convenient use of his political power for the furtherance upon advantageous terms of colonial railway enterprise to Kimberley and Rhodesia, the gross jobbery permitted to colleagues during his ministry which occasioned the resignation of Messrs. Rose-Innes, Merriman and Sauer, the purchase of Irish support in the House of Commons by a present of £10,000 to the party funds, when the Charter, conferring what were virtually sovereign rights over the entire hinterland of South Africa, was sought; the extraordinary combination of capacities which for a long period vested in one person the Premiership of Cape Colony, the Managing Directorship both of De Beers and of the Consolidated Goldfields, and the similar control of the Chartered Company, a combination which culminated in the Raid—this continuous testimony to the deliberate use of politics to further business ends, is the common property of all well-informed persons.

Where the State plays so large a part in the economic development of a country as has been the case in South Africa, where important concessions of lands and railways and laws affecting the supply of labour are constantly to the fore, it is natural enough that industrial and financial magnates should handle politics. Mr. Rhodes has never been an "Imperialist" in policy; he has steadily fought each real extension of "Imperial control," and, by skilful manipulation of Imperial powers and personnel, has succeeded up to the present time in using the money and the arms of Great Britain for the protection and furtherance of the business schemes upon which he and his fellow-directors have embarked. I do not hesitate to say that even now neither effective Imperial control nor effective popular representative government exists in Rhodesia, though elaborate provision is made for both. When business men enter politics in a country like South Africa they get what they want.

It is admitted that Mr. Rhodes did not play the part of a genuine "Imperialist" when in 1895 he planned a treacherous attack upon the Transvaal, abusing his position as a Minister of the Crown and wilfully deceiving the Imperial authorities. Failing by the awkwardness of his instrument he announced his intention to proceed henceforth by "Constitutional means." This expression was understood to signify that organised pressure would be exercised through the High Commissioner and the Colonial Secretary upon the Imperial power of Great Britain. Knowing the nature of the influences Mr. Rhodes and his friends could bring to bear, the South African Republic smelt the battle from afar and made those warlike preparations falsely represented as indicating an aggressive policy.

Does any single soul really believe that Messrs. Beit, Eckstein, Rouliot, Neumann, and the rest are Imperialists, or have any other aim than that of using the Imperial power to help them in their gold mining business? There are most urgent reasons why these gentlemen should seek the political control of the Transvaal. Let Mr. Fitzpatrick, late secretary of the Reform Committee, state what they were in 1896:

> "If you want the real grievances, they are: The Netherlands Railway Concession, the dynamite monopoly, the liquor traffic and native labour, which together constitute an unwarrantable burden of indirect taxation on the industry of two and a half million sterling annually.

Add to these one grievance, here omitted, that of the "bewaarplaatzen," or the question of the terms upon which the mine-owners shall obtain the mining rights on properties where they own at present only surface rights, and the whole matter lies in a nutshell. Mr. Fitzpatrick in this document, like Mr. Lionel Phillips, expressly excludes any interest in politics for any other purpose than the advance of profits in the mining industry. The whole matter is, indeed, more tersely summarised in the recently-published "Goldfields" annual report, in which reduction of working expenses and consequent increase of profits are contemplated as the result of the war.

These considerations make it evident that a small group of financial capitalists had large and definite advantages to gain by upsetting the Government of the Transvaal. It may be that other classes also stood to gain, the large, diffused investing public of Europe, the trading professional and labouring white population of the Rand. But the gains of these classes were very precarious; there is little to indicate that the general public of small investors will participate at all in the improved values of mining properties or in the speculative "boom" which will follow the "settlement." The shrewder tradesmen of Johannesburg and the great majority of miners are well aware that Eckstein and his fellows intend, by new "economies" in the working of the mines, the introduction of the Kimberley compound system or other methods of dispensing with local middlemen, and by the more effective control of the labour market, to keep to themselves as far as possible the economic gains of the new order. This reasonable suspicion explains why no large spontaneous enthusiastic agitation for coercion of the Transvaal Government arose among the rank and file of the Outlanders. Such real "grievances" as the latter felt were far from intolerable; there was no real danger to life, liberty or property, and the grosser abuses of taxation, finance and official maladministration did not fall with any considerable weight on them. The vast majority of all classes of the Outlander population lived a practically freer, a more enjoyable and a more prosperous life than they could have lived in any other place in the world. To any educated, "high-toned" visitor no doubt the civilisation of Johannesburg seemed crude, flash, materialistic and destitute of high ideals, but it was well adapted to the character and interests of the inhabitants. Almost every Johannesburger I met was enthusiastic in his admiration for the place; very few of them pretended to any personal grievances, though most of them within the last few years developed a fanatical desire that the Boer with whom they had virtually no personal contact, should be taught his proper place and should recognise the superiority of the rich commercial townsman.

. But granting that the real grievances were almost wholly economic and meant reduced profits of a few mining magnates, how far is it possible to trace the recent catastrophe in South Africa to the conscious policy of these men? In the mind of most English readers another accepted hypothesis blocks the way, the theory of a definite conspiracy aiming at the establishment of Dutch dominion throughout South Africa and imposing a deliberate aggressive policy upon the Republics. This is not the place to discuss the folly of attributing so fatuous a project to statesmen, many of whom, by education and professed sympathies, were closely attached to Great Britain, and who well knew both her power and her determination to defend her supremacy in South Africa. It is not of course impossible, though highly improbable, to represent Transvaal and Free State leaders as indulging in this wild dream and framing their national policy in accordance with such designs, hoping to consolidate for their attainment the united energies of the whole Dutch Africander population of South Africa. I do not question the *primâ facie* speciousness of this hypothesis: it correlates and seems to explain certain facts in the recent political conduct of the Transvaal. But I meet it by two arguments: first, that there is no direct substantial evidence in support of this hypothesis; secondly, that another hypothesis both gives a far better explanation of a larger number of facts and is sustained by irrefragible direct evidence.

I would challenge the upholders of the "Dutch Conspiracy" hypothesis to produce any evidence from the speech or conduct of the leading statesmen of the Republics, or of the admitted leaders of the Africander Bond, to prove the existence of any design to establish an independent Dutch Republic throughout South Africa. I do not assert that the idea may not have entered the mind of individual politicians, or that it may not have figured occasionally in the wilder rhetoric of political platforms. But no evidence exists that any responsible statesmen have ever seriously adopted this idea and moulded their policy upon it. The only so-called "evidence" adduced in support of this hypothesis is a certain set of facts which it professes to explain, such as the alleged overtures to Germany and other European Powers, the expenditure of a large secret service fund, and in particular the admitted large and growing expenditure of money upon forts, arms and ammunition. Such facts, it is maintained, are testimony to an aggressive design against the power of Great Britain. And this testimony would doubtless be valid, if there existed any independent evidence of this aggressive design. But no such evidence is forthcoming, and the hypothesis stands in the air—an unsubstantial surmise.

Now turn to our hypothesis of capitalist aggression, which, reversing the commonly accepted order of causation, explains the political and military preparations of the Transvaal as a distinctively defensive policy. This hypothesis is a *vera causa*, it rests upon a certain basis of admitted fact, and it affords a fuller and more consistent explanation of the actual order of events. Whatever be the exact estimate set upon the generous or prudential motives of the act of retrocession in 1881, no one would seriously maintain that Great Britain would have loosed her hold had the resources of Witwatersrand then been known. When the discoveries of gold were made in 1886, the Transvaal Government, having before their minds the fraudulent annexation of the diamond fields, that "most discreditable incident in British colonial history," as Mr. Froude described it, and the still more recent annexation of the neighbouring territories of Bechuanaland, began to fear for the "independence" of their country, and to make some defensive preparation.

Deprived, by the terms of the London Convention, of the right, exercised not only by independent States but by British colonies, of regulating and restricting foreign immigration, they watched with growing alarm the motley crowd of gold seekers who settled in ever-increasing numbers on the Rand. The race, character and conduct of this new population were utterly repellent to Boer nature and traditions. The new comers made no pretence of seeking a permanent home or of identifying themselves with the general interests of the body of citizens. They made no concealment of their aims: it was gold they sought; and when they began to ask for political rights it was with the evident and sole intention of using these rights for private gain and not for public good. Knowing that the political dominance of new citizens actuated by these motives meant the destruction of the political and social order of their State, the Transvaal Government sought to stem the tide, by obstructing the development of the gold industry which they could not crush, by erecting barriers to the attainment of the franchise, and by making some use of the power of taxation to prepare themselves against the armed attack which they had every reason to expect would some day be made upon them.

Before 1890 the restrictions set upon an unusually lax franchise were most moderate, and prohibited no genuine settler from gaining the political rights which he might seek. Neither was the public expenditure on armaments excessive for a people constantly exposed to border warfare, which required all its male inhabitants to be well equipped with arms. Not until the beginning of the present decade did the Transvaal adopt a strenuous policy of franchise restriction and armed preparation. Was this an offensive or a defensive policy? Let facts reply. In 1890 the new Census showed that the tide of immigration ran even faster than their fears; in 1891 the discovery of the extent and richness of the "deep levels," securing a long, secure and profitable future for the Rand gold-mines, and placing that future under the definite control of a single group of men, increased the alarm of the Transvaal Government. They foresaw a further increase in the rate of immigration and a stronger and more enduring motive for the "capitalists" to seek political control. The powerful Conservative Party in the State, led by Kruger, set itself stubbornly to defend the fortress of independence by new onerous restrictions on the franchise and by increased expenditure on arms. This party and this policy, though powerful, was not however at first dominant. There was a strong, genuine, Liberal movement among the burghers, which opposed the restrictive franchise policy and advocated an enlightened attitude towards the new-comers. In the Presidential election of 1893 Joubert, the leader of this party, was defeated only by a small majority: all the men of education were upon this side, the future was with them, and there was every prospect of their breaking down by natural processes of education the blind, fanatical obstruction of the old Boer party.

This promise of internal reform was suddenly blighted by the Outlander policy, which culminated in the Jameson Raid. This event was not quite the "bolt from the blue" which it is sometimes represented to be. Ever since the establishment of the Transvaal Republican Union at Barberton in 1887, revolutionary forces had been gathering among the Outlanders. The formation of the Chamber of Mines in 1889, and the National Union three years later, gave definiteness to the political ambitions of the "capitalists." However "Constitutional" the immediate attitude of the mining capitalists might be, the unscrupulous corruption they adopted to gain their ends, and the knowledge that complete attainment of these ends meant a practical subjection of the political machinery to the requirements of the mines, were calculated to increase rather than allay alarm. At the close of 1894, a year before the Raid, the language of the active mining capitalists became bolder and assumed a distinctly minatory tone in their negociations with the Government. It is in this year that we first trace a notable increase in the "Special Expenditure" of the Government, doubtless attributable to a growing reasonable feeling of alarm. Not, however, until 1896 do we find that large, constantly-growing increase of expenditure upon war preparations which is falsely attributed to the "aggressive" policy of the Transvaal. There had no doubt been a large rise in military expenditure ever since 1885, but this is explained by the dictates of reasonable caution on the one hand and by the increase of State resources on the other. Every department of expenditure had increased with the increase of the national income: the growth of expenditure on hospitals, education, police and other peaceable services, is quite as noticeable as the growth of "special expenditure" and "War Department expenses." Prior to 1895 there is no evidence whatever on which to convict the Transvaal Government of an "aggressive policy." Her fears of the Outlander we may well consider to have been exaggerated, her obstructive policy unwise, her armed preparations needless and liable to be misinterpreted. But keeping in mind alike the ignorance, the prejudices and the past experience of the Boers, we cannot refuse to consider that their policy was undertaken for purposes of defence.

When the Jameson Raid took place, those fears were justified, and the effect upon the enlightened, progressive party in the State was most disastrous. It was now idle for any burgher to preach liberal concessions, or to advocate drastic internal reforms. This Raid, condemned only for its failure by the vast majority of the British in South Africa, virtually condoned by the British Government, was a terrible setback to the cause of peaceful reform within the Transvaal. Was it unnatural that the Boers should fear lest this semi-official attack upon their independence, organised by a combination of mining capitalists and British politicians, including, as they commonly believe, the connivance of the Colonial Secretary himself, should be followed by subsequent better organised and, more formidable attempts? All the factors of danger still remained, more powerful and exasperated by one failure. Ever since the Raid, the agitators of Johannesburg and their Press have made no concealment of their intention to gain their end by constitutional or unconstitutional means. The provocative tone of the communications of Sir A. Milner and Mr. Chamberlain, whether justified or not by actual events, was interpreted as the prelude to a convenient quarrel, which was to attain the object which the Raid had failed to win. I do not defend the discretion of the Transvaal policy or the correctness of their interpretation of British diplomacy: I merely insist that the attitude adopted by them was taken up as a defensive and not as an offensive policy. They saw since 1895 the same men who had planned the Raid, animated by the same motives and possessing even greater financial and political resources. They watched each step in the political game: they saw appointed to the post of High Commissioner a man of strong "Imperialistic" proclivities, who fell quickly under the control of politicians, financiers and journalists, whom they knew to be their enemies. They saw the concentration of economic power in the Chamber of Mines: the men who held this power they saw financing and otherwise supporting the South African League, a body expressly devoted to the establishment of the "Supremacy of Great Britain in South Africa." More important still, they saw these men buying, not for commercial but for propagandist purposes, the most important organs of the Press in the colony, and establishing at great expense new organs of revolutionary agitation in Johannesburg: they saw public opinion throughout South Africa poisoned by the mendacity of this unscrupulous Press, visibly operated in collusion so as to arouse public passion and to drive the British Imperial policy towards a catastrophe. Seeing all this, and knowing, on the one hand the power, the motives and the methods of Mr. Rhodes and his fellow-capitalists, on the other the personal animus, the ambition and the remarkable energy of Mr. Chamberlain, was it unnatural that the Transvaal Government should contemplate as a certainty some early attack upon the independence of their country, and should reject suggestions of a policy of liberal concessions as a mere postponement of the inevitable attack?

This was their fatalist interpretation of coming events: they knew the character and objects of the men engineering the assault, that nothing short of the complete political and economic control of the country would satisfy them, and they determined to make such preparations as would enable them to sell their liberties dearly. Such is the hypothesis which gives the best and fullest explanation of the facts.

This analysis of the case of Capitalism using Imperialism is of necessity imperfect. No play of historic forces is so simple as this has been represented to be. I have abstracted and assigned dramatic prominence to the self-seeking motives and energy of financial capitalists. I have done so because I believe that in this, and in other cases of aggressive Imperialism, this factor, though it never acts alone, is the most powerful guiding force, co-operating with and moulding for its own purpose other weaker forces with purer but less definite aims. Just as the ambition of the Rand capitalists finds a certain genuine movement of political reform operated by middle-class enthusiasts and uses it, so it coalesces with and "engineers" the medley of aims and feelings to which the term Imperialism is commonly applied. Though no exact definition of the nature and objects of Imperialism is possible, it contains certain clearly distinguishable threads of thought and feeling. Among these certain genuinely social and humane motives stand prominent: the desire to promote the causes of civilisation and Christianity, to improve the economic and spiritual condition of lower races, to crush slavery and to bring all parts of the habitable world into closer material and moral union. These motives are real and enter into Imperialism: they are its redeeming factors, but they are not its most powerful directing forces. So long as we regard Imperialism as a broad, general principle these higher and better ideas and feelings take front rank: but when we descend from principle to practice it is quite different. If we turn to our present concrete instance, and ask what is the real Imperialism which goes forth to aid and abet the Capitalism which we have analysed, we shall discover to our chagrin that this Imperialism is in large measure resolvable into capitalist or profit-seeking influences. The driving forces of aggressive Imperialism are the organised influences of certain professional and commercial classes which have certain definite economic advantages to gain by assuming this pseudo-patriotic cloak. The most potent of all these influences, the power behind the throne in every modern civilised country, is the financier, the home representative of that very class whose operations "on the spot" I have analysed above. The power of this class, exerted directly upon politicians, or indirectly through the Press upon public opinion, is perhaps the most serious problem in public life to-day. The hammering of Kruger at the Stock Exchange is a concise and most luminous revelation of this central truth. But this nucleus of economic force in "Imperialism" gathers around it certain other allied economic interests.

The powerfully-organised iron and shipbuilding trades, with many related industries, are direct and large gainers by public expenditure upon armaments which this sort of Imperialism necessitates : most of the large export trades are won over by fallacious appeals to the Trade which "follows the Flag." The "Services" offer the cleanest and most natural support to an aggressive foreign policy : expansion of the empire appeals powerfully to the aristocracy and the professional classes by offering new and ever-growing fields for the honourable and profitable employment of their sons. The general body of the investing public is easily persuaded to use the resources of the State in order to safeguard and appreciate their private investments in foreign lands.

These strong definite economic interests are the principal propellers of aggressive Imperialism, consciously or instructively using, in order to conceal their selfish dominance, the generous but often mistaken impulses of humanitarian sentiment, and relying in the last resort upon one powerful secret ally which ever lurks in the recesses of the national character. This ally is that race-lust of dominance, that false or inverted patriotism which measures the glory of its country by another's shame, and whose essential immorality is summed up in the doctrine that British paramountcy is a "right." It is to this blind and brutal lust that our financiers made their final and successful appeal, when they instructed their Press and their political tools to so falsify the wholesome Africander sentiment as to make it appear a Dutch challenge to British ascendancy throughout South Africa. This British Imperial passion, once roused upon both Continents, responded with eager frenzy to the mandates of the masters who had invoked it and who seek to employ it for their gain. Mr. Chamberlain, the faithful representative of this Imperialism, possibly imagines himself a free agent, and possibly designs to use for purposes of personal and Imperial aggrandisement the economic forces of South African finance. But the generals of finance well know he is their instrument and not they his : they are the men upon the spot who know what they want and mean to get it. The apparent spontaneity of Imperialism is a mere illusion : its forces obey the stimulus and the direction of financial masters.

Those who reject this analysis, with the stress it lays upon distinctively economic initiative, because it appears crude in its simplicity, do wrong. The apparent complexity of such an issue is only superficial, for the most part fabricated and serving as a screen for the play of a few simple, primitive, selfish forces.   Times change, men do not greatly change.   The memorable saying of Sir Thomas More is still applicable in our day: "Everywhere do I perceive a certain conspiracy of rich men seeking their private advantage under the name and pretext of the Commonweal."

J. A. HOBSON.

Article 4

THE INNER MEANING OF PROTECTIONISM.

CONVINCED Free Traders are too prone to explain the survival of, or the reversion to, Protection by the greed of a few dominant industrial interests and the short-sighted policy of the masses, who prefer indirect to direct taxes, and are easily persuaded that other people pay them. Protection, moreover, makes its appeal to the producer, professing to safeguard his interests, and, though every producer is likewise a consumer, the former function is more exigent: a promise of high wages carries more weight than a threat of high prices, because the average man looks more closely to his earnings than to his expenditure.

But behind all this there lie two tendencies and two sentiments relating to them which Free Traders have ignored. Free Trade makes no provision to secure that industry and an industrial population shall remain attached to any particular piece of earth. On the contrary, the assumption is that both capital and labour shall easily transfer themselves from the place which they have hitherto occupied to any other portion of the industrial world where they can earn higher profits or wages, and that it is desirable they should do so. Thus inside the "Free Trade" area of England itself, the forces of the Industrial Revolution took away the important textile industry of the Eastern counties, transferring it to Lancashire, and destroyed the flourishing iron industry of Sussex and Kent, absorbing it in the new industries upon the Northern and Midland coal fields. If this suckage of trade and population may happen from the free play of natural economic forces within this or any other country, may we not expect a similar result from a grouping of countries, trading with one another as freely as the different parts of England trade with one another? Where capital and labour can pass quickly, easily and cheaply, from one country to another, what is there to prevent a nation, whose land is less well adapted to modern industrial requirements than other nations with which she is in close commercial intercourse, from being stripped of large portions of her trade and her industrial population? There is no guarantee under Free Trade that any single industry or any single industrial population shall stay permanently fixed in the political area termed Great Britain. What is there to ensure the continuance of the great staple, textile, metal and other manufactures in these isles, supposing that the world-competition, upon which we are now entering, makes it evident that the capital and labour they employ can be more profitably employed elsewhere, in America, in India or China? Or, if the labour will not flow so easily or so quickly on to the best area of employment, the capital will go and leave it impotent for industry. Many Protectionists are persuaded that the relative advantages for manufactures and commerce, which England possessed during the greater part of the 19th century, are disappearing, and that other nations, by cheaper or more industrious labour, greater enterprise in organisation and invention, or easier access to raw materials, have undermined our industrial prosperity. These competitive forces, often assisted by foreign fiscal policy, if they are allowed to operate without resistance on our part, may serve to drain Great Britain of much of her most profitable manufacturing and commercial enterprise. Now Free Trade doctrine and practices offer no resistance to such a movement. According to Free Trade, if the soil, climate, position and other natural conditions of these islands no longer offer sufficient inducements to retain capital and labour in employment thus, they should be free to flow elsewhere: the work of the world must and ought to be done wherever it can be done most cheaply and most efficiently. Free Trade, in a word, stands for the maximum production of world-wealth and for the largest remuneration of capital and labour engaged in producing it, but is regardless of the *locale* upon which this wealth is produced and consumed. Free Trade assumes internationalism.

Now the Protectionist, taking his stand on national patriotism, is seriously concerned to keep as much industry and as large a population as possible within the limits of these islands; and our Imperial Protectionist of to-day is willing to place restrictions upon foreign trade in order to keep within the limits of the British Empire a large population, who shall earn a living wage for their labour and a living profit on their capital.

The most important change in modern history is the growing severance between the political and the industrial limits of national life: as a political unit a British citizen is confined in his interests to these isles, as an industrial unit he may be far more closely identified with China, South America, or Russia. This severance between political and industrial interests everywhere seems to threaten political solidarity, and sets up two tendencies, Imperialism and Protection. Imperialism represents a more or less conscious and organised effort of a nation to expand its old political boundaries, and to take in by annexation other outside countries where its citizens have acquired strong industrial interests. Protection represents the converse tendency, an effort to prevent industrial interests from wandering outside the political limits of the nation, to keep capital and labour employed within the political area, confining extra-national relations to commerce within the narrower limits of the term. Modern Conservatism, concerned for the territorial integrity of national life, pursues both policies, expanding political control, contracting industrial life, in order to try and preserve the identity of the politics and industry of its citizens. It represents the struggle of a deformed and belated nationalism against the growing spirit which everywhere is breaking through the old national limits and is laying the economic foundation for the coming inter-nationalism.

This is the inner meaning of the new wave of Protectionism in England. Its adherents fear lest England's natural advantages of soil, climate, position, labour-power and business-enterprise should not suffice in the turmoil of keen world-competition to keep enough industry within our national or imperial soil. The traditional policy of game-preserving impels them to have recourse to similar methods of preserving trade within the ring-fence of the national or imperial dominions.

Along with this sentiment works an allied sentiment of self-sufficiency. It is not enough that Great Britain should keep a large volume of industry within her shores : she must defend herself against another implication of Free Trade, an excessive division of world-labour, which, by specialising the work of a nation, robs it of self-sufficiency. Even if Great Britain is strong enough to retain her fair share of world-industry, Free Trade, by confining British industry more and more to certain specific branches of manufacture and commerce, increases her dependence for the prime necessaries of national life upon the good will and regular industry of other nations. When a nation depends for the supply of its daily bread upon the economic activity of other nations, its political independence is felt to be imperilled. Whatever be the advantage of international division of labour at ordinary times, it is felt that the national unit should, at any rate, not so far commit herself to specialised industry that she cannot, upon an emergency, resume the power to supply herself with food and other necessaries of life from her own resources.

Protectionism, interpreted in the light of these apprehensions, is an endeavour to struggle against certain dangers inherent in the world-economy of Free Trade, and to keep within the territorial limits of the nation a sufficient volume and an adequate variety of industry.

Now the Free Trader has several answers to this line of argument. Admitting that it is theoretically possible for trade to shrink in volume within the national area, as a result of free world-competition, he will deny that Great Britain is in fact subjected to this process. An impregnable array of evidence can be adduced to prove that our industrial prosperity is waxing and not waning; that the diminution of certain old industries is attended by a more than proportionate growth of new industries; that the more rapid recent development of such countries as Germany and the United States is on the whole a source of strength, not of weakness, to our powers of national production; that certain particular injuries inflicted by the rivalry of nations are more than compensated by the indirect benefits of a more effective international co-operation. Every increase of the productive power of Germany and the United States is a source of increased wealth to Great Britain, just in proportion as the growing volume of our commerce with these countries obliges them to hand over to us, by ordinary processes of exchange, an increased quantity of their enhanced national wealth.

These commonplaces of the theory of free exchange are ignored by the fearful hosts of Protection.

As for the danger attributed to specialisation of industry which makes us dependent upon other nations for our food supply, the argument, so far as it carries any weight, relies on political rather than economic considerations. If there were any reason to expect a general conspiracy of foreign wheat-growing nations so blinded to their obvious self-interest as to establish a trade boycott against Great Britain, in such a case a policy of artificial stimulation of agriculture within the Empire, though involving a great sacrifice of aggregate national wealth, would be defensible if it could be shown to be efficacious. But even here the Protectionist case collapses when from theory we resort to fact. For when we regard the amount of our dependence upon the United States and other foreign countries for our food and other necessaries of life, we shall perceive that we have gone too far in our international reliance for any such reversion to Imperial self-sufficiency to be efficacious. An endeavour to stimulate by artificial means the development of British and Imperial agriculture for purposes of self-support, while it would cost us dear, could not succeed within any reasonable time in securing us against the necessity of buying food from those foreign nations whom we are called upon to distrust. We should merely offend them without securing our economic independence. The politics of such a course would be even worse than its economics.

But the deepest defect of the new Protectionism lies in its utter inadequacy to achieve its end. For if that end is to secure the retention of a sufficient volume and variety of industry and of industrial population within the territorial limits of the kingdom or the empire, the sort of protection which is now proposed will be quite incompetent to compass it.

This can easily be seen. The result of the specialisation of national industry under Free Trade (however imperfect or " one-sided ") is to enhance the productivity of the capital and labour engaged in it. An artificial restriction of this process of specialisation must therefore be attended by a diminution of the general productivity of capital and labour. The instructed Protectionist will hardly question this. Either he will admit a reduction of aggregate national wealth, defending it on the ground of greater variety and increased self-sufficiency : or he will assert that a larger employment of capital and labour will enable the same quantity of wealth to be produced as before. It matters not which line of argument is taken, the fact remains that the result of Protection will be a diminished productivity of capital and labour *per unit*. This must be attended by a general shrinkage in the rate of profits and of wages, a process accelerated by the fact that rent of land will take a larger share of the total diminished national income. Now, if profits and wages fall, both capital and labour will tend to seek employment outside the protected area, in foreign lands : the fact that protective systems prevail in these foreign lands, not being a new factor in the situation, is immaterial. So, even if it be argued that an increased volume of employment of capital and labour might directly ensue from a protective tariff, that capital and labour, obtaining a lower rate of real remuneration, will not stay within the protected national area, but will tend to seek the more remunerative outside employment. This theory is supported by innumerable concrete evidences.

Protection, by lowering the average productiveness of capital and labour, tends to expel them from the protected area. Capital, more fluid, leaves more easily and quickly : labour lags, and a grave condition of " unemployment " embarrasses the situation : eventually labour too migrates in order to co-operate with its necessary economic adjunct. Can Protection stop this process of migration which plainly defeats its end by exasperating the very disease it is designed to cure ? Yes, provided it is sufficiently thorough. Protection, to be effective, must not stand upon the feeble expedients of preferential or even prohibitive tariffs aimed against the import of foreign goods. It must support this barrier by a second barrier, prohibiting the export of British capital and British labour. The more rigorous Protection of the 17th and 18th centuries took what steps in this direction were then necessary, by restriction or prohibition of the export of machinery and skilled labour. More rigorous protective measures would now be needed. For the fluidity of monetary investments in foreign lands was then a *négligeable* factor : whereas it is the factor of first significance in modern world industry. In order then for our new Protectionists to gain their object of setting back the tide of industrial internationalism, so as to achieve the economic solidarity and self-sufficiency of the British Empire, they must devise means of preventing fluid capital and labour from leaving the country. Unless they see their way to carry Protection thus far, they will behold their policy of protective and retaliatory tariffs reduced to nullity by the free play of the enlightened self-interest of capital and labour seeking elsewhere the employment now rendered unprofitable within the British Empire.

Nothing short of this protective policy of " thorough," making for the well-nigh complete economic isolation of our Empire, by a virtual prohibition, not only of imports but of exports, can avail to safeguard the nation against the imaginary perils of a Free Trade economy which is only the industrial aspect of the slowly-growing internationalism with which lies the future of civilisation.

Protectionism, thus interpreted, is the expression of a false spirit of patriotism seeking to confine industry within a national or imperial area, so as to defend the nation, or the empire, against what it regards as the disintegrating influences of commercial internationalism.

Now this patriotism is doubly false as expressed in that form of preferential Protectionism now before our country. In the first place, if carried into effect, it would injure our national life by narrowing the stream of intercourse with other nations, upon which in the future, as in the past, the growth and enrichment of our nationality depend. It is no better for a nation than for a man to live alone, and the economic self-sufficiency, at which Protection aims, could it be achieved, would deprive our national industry and our national life of those new supplies of foreign stock and stimuli which have played so large a part in building the very industries which we have come to regard as characteristically British. The greatness of English manufacture and commerce is so demonstrably due to the free receptivity of England : so many of her industries are the direct product of Flemish, Italian, French and German skill and invention, drawn into our country by our industrial and political practice of the open door, that any stoppage of this liberty of foreign access, such as must attend any substantial measure of Protectionism, would inflict the gravest damage upon a main source of our national industrial growth. Even more detrimental would be the diminution of all forms of higher intercourse which this lessening of commercial intercourse must involve. Ideas always follow trade routes, and a limitation of international trade will restrict the free flow of ideas and feelings between Great Britain and foreign nations, and will throw us more and more upon the restricted intellectual resources of our empire. It is not extravagant to suggest that we have more to learn from France, Germany and America than from Australasia and South Africa ; and that if it were a case of making immediate economic sacrifices, it would pay us better as a nation in the long run to maintain a free expansive intercourse with foreign civilised nations than to cultivate a process of narrow, intellectual inter-breeding within the British Empire. As matters stand, our immediate economic interests are so plainly identical with the wider, higher interests of our national civilisation that the proposed change of commercial policy would inflict a double blow upon our national life.

Hardly less injurious to true nationalism is the attempt, which underlies a preferential tariff, to merge the national life of Great Britain, as a political and economic unit, in the Empire. The natural tendency of recent history has been towards a free development of a distinctively national spirit and institutions in Australasia, Canada and South Africa, expressing itself in liberty of fiscal policy, as well as in a stricter limitation of the forms and substance of political control by the Mother Country. This movement is not to be regarded as making for the dissolution of the Empire, but as a natural expression of a certain local specialisation of interests in new forms of self-government within the Empire: this liberty of growing new political organs with increasing differentiation of functions is necessary to the health of the body politic. Every manifestation of genuine regard for the Mother Country in our self-governing Colonies must be rightly understood as a testimony to the success of this " simple system of natural liberty " which has ruled the relations of Great Britain to her Colonies during several generations. Any attempt artificially to draw closer the economic or the political bonds impedes this growth of wholesome " nationalism " in the Colonies, while it weakens British nationalism by making it diffuse and amorphous. With an Englishman who is to be described as genuinely " patriotic," England stands first, the British Empire next; with an Australian, Australia first, the British Empire next, and so with the Canadian or the South African. Even were it possible, it would be supremely unwise to try to dissipate this narrower nationalism by merging it into imperialism; and the attempt, artificially, to force this merger is more likely than any other course to defeat its object by driving our Colonies to seek expression for their growing sentiments and interests of nationality outside the political area of the British Empire.

The endeavour to enlarge the scope of British nationalism, and correspondingly to break the narrower force of Colonial nationalism, by spreading it over the vast heterogeneous area of the British Empire, implies a fatal misunderstanding of the meaning and uses of nationalism. Such a nationalism would be unintelligent, unstable, and, on the part of our self-governing Colonies, recalcitrant; for they would find their separate self-interests, which in spite of the nominal merger would endure, continually thwarted by a policy imposed upon them by the dominant partner, in her own interest or that of the dumb portion of the Empire which would form her peculiar charge. It could never be the true interest of any of our self-governing Colonies to enter a closer imperial federation with a Mother Country that is saddled with our vast burden of non-self-governing possessions. In spirit and in policy colonialism is the antithesis of imperialism; and the rising nationality of our self-governing Colonies must revolt against the perilous and unprofitable burden of this " unfree " Empire.

Thus the modified Protectionism of the preferential tariff is an attempt to fight against the spirit of internationalism by a method which actually undermines the genuine forces of nationalism.

All the wanton waste and mischief of this movement arises from the false conception of nationalism which deems it the enemy of internationalism. The true friend of internationalism, as distinguished from the more amorphous cosmopolitan, most urgently desires the maintenance of nationalism, and, as a means to effective nationalism, would maintain that full free intercourse of local areas which contributes to the making of powerful nationality by transfusion of blood, ideas and sentiments.

Free Trade is essential to this nationalism, and thence derives much not only of its economic, but of its ethical validity.

It has been a fashion to deride Cobdenism for two diametrically opposite reasons. Some have disparaged it for its huxter ethics, its excessive reliance upon materialistic bonds of trade, which ignored all the deeper-rooted forces of national or racial sentiment. Others reproached it for its Utopian idealism, its conviction that peace and goodwill were the really dominant forces of humanity, concealed by merely superficial rivalry on the political and commercial planes : knock down tariffs, reduce armaments, show faith in the latent powers of national good-will, an early millennium would ensue.

It is now argued that events have proved the falsity of Cobdenism. But this argument shows a failure to grasp the meaning of commercial internationalism as taught by Cobden. In the first place, we have never practised more than one-half of Cobden's policy. Cobden would have us test the commercial and moral forces of internationalism by ceasing to rely upon military force and territorial aggression for the advance of commerce. Imperialism implies the inhibition of those very forces upon which Cobden most explicitly relied for the success of his internationalism. Secondly, so far as the real cause of internationalism has made advance, this advance has been directly proportionate to the growth of international trade, and has been impeded by every tariff that has checked this trade.

What Cobden's analysis failed to recognise was that an appeal made, as was his, to the collective self-interests of whole nations, is only completely effective where the government expresses the aggregate interests of the nation, that it is liable to fail where the interests of special classes or industries within the nation arrogate to themselves the powers of government. The full efficacy of Cobdenism implies the existence of industrial democracies. By an industrial democracy I signify not merely a government of the people by the people for the people, instead of a government of the people by the boss for the millionaire, but also a free play of economic forces which secures to the people, as a whole, the increased consumption of wealth rendered possible by each improvement in the development of natural resources and of the arts of production.

It is quite evident that one prime direct cause of the adoption of tariffs has been the increasing difficulty manufacturers experience in disposing of their wares at profitable prices in the home or neutral markets. This general tendency towards over-production of manufactured goods, and often even of food and raw materials, common and almost chronic among the increasing number of nations that have entered the modern era of mechanical industry, is only intelligible upon one hypothesis. Since all trade is ultimately an exchange of commodities, everything that is produced can obviously be sold and consumed; for someone possesses a corresponding power to buy whatever is produced. If therefore it is in point of fact so much more difficult to sell than to buy, that the power to produce has continually to be kept in check, this curious phenomenon can only be explained by imputing to those who have the power to consume a refusal of the exercise of that power. This refusal of a full application of the power to purchase and consume is itself only explicable as part of the wider phenomenon of mal-distribution of wealth in modern societies. In a well-ordered society every increase in the power of production would automatically be attended by a corresponding rise in the general standard of consumption, wants rising to correspond with every enhanced power to satisfy them. In such societies there could be no apparent over-production (outside the range of minor miscalculation), and therefore no difficulty in finding markets. The only economic explanation of the growing struggle for markets that stimulates Protection is an unsound condition of economic order which prevents the peoples from absorbing freely in their rising standard of consumption all the growing wealth made possible by scientific methods of production. Since the same phenomenon of mal-distribution of economic power within the nation alone explains how in every nation, irrespective of its form of government, the actual control of the fiscal policy is exercised by strong groups of industrial politicians in the interests of special trades, it becomes quite evident how Protectionism is rooted in the larger social question. So far as Cobdenism has failed, it is from no inherent defect of the doctrine or its practice, but from wider causes which have hitherto prevented the emergence of a really democratic fiscal policy even in those nations that have clothed themselves with the forms of democracy. Protectionism is always likely to survive or to recur in nations where class interests, of land owners, of export manufacturers, the military services, and their industrial parasites, remain politically strong enough to push their group-interests to the detriment of the commonwealth. Until the people get a larger control over the industrial resources of the country, an increased power of consumption, they cannot checkmate the power of the industrial oligarchy, which is continually liable to use protective tariffs so as to divert into their own pockets an increasing share of the reduced aggregate wealth of the nation.

It seems as if industrial democracy must precede political democracy, so as to make the latter possible. But it is not difficult to turn the issue round and show that certain changes of political machinery are essential to the attainment of any measure of real industrial democracy. So we seem to be involved in a vicious circle. But the circle is not really vicious: it is rather a type of the perfect harmony which must exist in the play of progressive forces. The true democracy is neither political nor industrial, but both in one, and the progressive forces which make for its attainment are the same. The chain of logic runs thus: without economic justice there can be no democracy; democracy is the essence of true nationalism; Free Trade is the expression of national self-interests through the intercourse of nations, and is thus the foundation of internationalism.

I have shown that Preferential Tariffs, Fair Trade, or other interferences with liberty of imports are Protection, and that Protection is economically injurious, first to the weaker classes of the nation, the working classes, secondly to the nation as a whole, thirdly to the industrial world or to economic internationalism.

But the heaviest count of the indictment against Protectionism is that it attempts to cancel the conditions of international morality: not merely is it an organised formal assertion of that national selfishness which degrades patriotism from a sentiment of inclusive affection to one of external animosity, but it shuts the door to the free entrance of those foreign goods which are the material expression of foreign life and the first foundation of higher intercourse, a better understanding and a finer feeling between nations.

International trade is the incipient form, the true utilitarian condition, of international morality: trade-intercourse is the beginning of human fellowship.

The Imperialist policy of political expansion and its natural ally, the Protectionist policy of commercial contraction, are both enemies of international morality, in that they destroy the free self expression and intercourse of nations.

The civilisation of the future demands the maintenance of strong independent nations—fearless of aggression—entering into ever closer commercial intercourse with one another, and, in the practice of mutual aid upon the plane of physical life, laying the foundation of a higher spiritual fellowship. Neither political expansion nor industrial contraction can do aught else than offer mischievous and ultimately impotent impediments to this course of world-civilisation, which, so far from endangering nationalism, strengthens and enriches it by placing it in strong organic harmony with the life of other nations.

J. A HOBSON.

Article 5

THE ETHICS OF INTERNATIONALISM.*

It may, I think, be rightly said that the greatest thing which has happened within the last two generations has been the practical enlargement of the world for all members of civilized communities. The world, of course, is of a different size for all of us, and it is very largely determined in that size by the attitude, the conscious and the unconscious attitude which we adopt towards it. That is to say, the world is as large as we by our practical experience and our imaginative experience and sympathy choose and are able to make it. Perhaps it is difficult for us to realize how small a thing the world meant for most of our grandfathers and grandmothers, living in an age when their practicable movements and actual concrete ex-

---

* An address before the Society for Ethical Culture of Philadelphia.

periences of life were confined almost entirely to a minute fraction of the soil of the particular country upon which they were born. Even in this country, where movement was freer and larger at that time, it may be said that the world was not one tenth or one hundredth part so great, if measured by the experience of the citizen of fifty years ago, as it is for you to-day.

We know, of course, in general terms, how this change has been brought about. Partly, it is due to the facilitation of travel, the direct contact and experience with other peoples spreading so widely among modern developed nations—at any rate so far as the more wealthy classes are concerned. But that is not the chief instructor and the chief enlarger of the world. It is through the facilitation of news, through the press and the telegraph service, that we are brought to-day into ever closer, more immediate and sympathetic contact with the whole world. Everyone, to-day, as we say familiarly, lives at the end of a telegraph line, which means not merely that all the great and significant happenings in the world are brought to his attention in a way which was impossible a generation or two ago, but that they are brought at once and simultaneously to the attention of great masses of people, so that anything happening in the most remote part of the world makes its immediate impression upon the society of nations. The whole world is made cognizant of it, and the immediate and simultaneous sympathy it arouses brings a new element of sociality into the world. In this sense we may say that the world has been recently discovered for the mass of civilized mankind. It has been brought effectively within the true area of their attention.

But what is the intellectual and moral attitude to-day toward this large world, broken as it still remains into a large number of so-called separate nations? We are hardly prepared to take a cool, clear, scientific view of international relations. The press, of which I spoke just now, throws the limelight now upon one corner of the world, now upon another; now it is perhaps upon South Africa, now it is upon some great stir in China, again, some South American rebellion occupies the field of immediate attention, then we are swept away to the mystery

of Russia, to street fights in the city of Moscow, to the erup-
tion of some volcano, or some new atrocities up on the Congo.
Such interest so broken cannot be said to be effectively scientific
or effectively humanitarian.   We are not able to adjust clearly
our minds or our sympathetic feelings to the interests of
humanity as disclosed by these great events.   This rapid, sensa-
tional posing of the different portions of the world before us
seems at present to dissipate rather than integrate our thought
and feeling, to arouse a constant, quick succession of unrelated
interests.   The daily press, the chief instrument of this dissipa-
tion is engaged continually in trying to alarm, surprise and
amaze us by strongly marked display of new incidents in different portions of the world.   What we call the "yellow" press (a
press which is not confined to your country, a press which is
closely imitated in my own country and in various countries of
Europe), seems to have developed a new idea of providence,
presenting it in the character of a great sporting committee,
engaged in arranging "events" over the world; great feats, great
new international handicaps are commonly being announced
in alarmist letters, and this press, of course, is primarily engaged
in taking the gate-money for this class of variety entertainment.   So far as the conscious will of man is concerned, so far
as these great events which are taking place in different parts
of the world are the products of individual will, the notion is
not wholly illusory.   Underneath those motives which are
brought forward to explain what is happening in political and
other fields of enterprise, underlying such terms as "honor"
and "prestige," we have the struggle for spheres of influence
among nations, the struggle for greatness, for national sel
assertion in various forms and in various parts of the world,
that struggle which in its political and military side takes the
title of imperalism.   It is this contest that occupies the chief
attention of the international committee, for which Mr. Roose-
velt and Kaiser Wilhelm are informal secretaries.   For while
many of the more violent and surprising happenings in the
world present themselves to the reading public as uncaused
sensations, the highest interest attaches to their great bouts of
organized adventure, in which the power of personalities plays

a most distinguished and dramatic part. For "movements" and "forces" cannot even in the most democratic countries displace individual personality in the interpretation of history: in the most modern times national "destinies" are still frequently swayed by the personal influence of some great swashbuckler or some gambler like the great Napoleon III in France, or some calculating statesman like Prince Bismarck. Such men with such passions still play a considerable part in determining the great movements of nations. But, of course, in explaining history, we must not be led back into the old, false, heroic method of interpretation. We must recognize that behind these personalities are certain wider plays of interest and passion, the interests and passions of classes or groups within a nation, or the play of the desires, ambitions and needs of whole peoples. To these great forces, guided and exploited perhaps to some extent by the ambitions of strong men, statesmen and generals of industry or war, we must look if we should seek to understand the modern development of history. Not merely does the interest we have in foreign nations grow greater in modern times, but it is equally evident that the actual influences which work upon the lives of all of us from distant parts of the world are multiplying very fast. It is a familiar truth that whether we look to industry, to politics, to science, to literature, to travel, we find a number of bonds of interest which band men together irrespective of the national limits of the country to which they belong and in which they are born. Even so little time as a generation ago it might be said that for the most part we lived alone as nations; nations were loosely related to one another, and their individual members therefore, had a very slight realization of what the world meant outside their own particular nation.

Now is it equally obvious that every great public issue which confronts us in life is international; it is impossible to trace down those issues which are presented to us as great social issues, political or economic, and to find any solution which is satisfactory that does not present the elements of internationality. If any of you are sympathetically engaged in any great task of modern social reform you will find that you are constantly brought up against this fact; you cannot find a solution adequate for the particular problem upon which you are concentrating your attention that is not thwarted by the play of forces outside your own nationality. That of course is conspicuously true of those movements associated with capital and labor, and indeed all movements which are comprised under the term "The Social Problem." It is not possible, we are now coming to see, for a social problem to be solved by a single nation; no nation can advance toward its solution at a very much faster pace than other nations, nor can it solve what it calls its own problems itself. There are no large problems which are securely fastened within the confines of a single nationality. All attempts to make this national isolation are in the long run futile. If we attempt to interrupt what is happening in the world to-day, we find the key to that interpretation in the tendency to equalization of the material, intellectual and moral resources over the face of the earth. This comes home to us most clearly in commercial matters, in the play of commerce between nation and nation. A generation ago that play was very slight. Now, of course, great masses of commodities are flowing tolerably freely, in spite of tariffs, over the whole surface of the globe. New countries are coming continually into the area of effective commercial intercourse. But that perhaps is not the most significant aspect of the material change which is taking place. The productive powers of mankind, capital and labor, are flowing with incomparably greater freedom over the whole world. The modern methods of investment simply mean that huge masses of capital are moving about to find the spot where they can combine most effectively with natural resources and with labor, and labor is seeking to follow the same line of free flow. This is the great thing which is happening from the standpoint of material development of the earth, the flow of capital and labor, drawn primarily by the self-interest of its owners to combine in methods and at places which are most effective for the production of wealth for the world—not of wealth for any individual nation. This flow of capital and labor, the largest practical thing that is happening to-day, is in its real meaning directed to the production and distribution of wealth over the world, and all these little laws which are set up by nationalities to regulate the kind of things that shall come from one country to another, and the way in which they shall enter, and the terms upon which capital shall be used in foreign nations, and the regulations which restrict the movements of the flow of labor from one nation to another, all these are small and comparatively trivial barriers set up against this majestic world-flow of capital and labor. What is aimed at is a leveling process throughout the world, a leveling of economic and ultimately of social conditions between one part of the world and another; and the forces which impel this great movement are immensely and immeasurably stronger than those which artificial barriers of national law can possibly set up to prohibit or restrain them. You may, of course, impede the particular flow, you may alter a little the direction, you may block certain channels, but you cannot effectively, to any considerable degree, control these great world forces. It is the pace and the intricacy of this new movement which is causing a great deal of the bewilderment and the impotence which mark the conduct of modern statesmen in all the countries of the world.

The modes of cosmopolitanism which are already established strike us often as most significant. You can book a passage by rail or sea in London or New York for any point in the civilized or uncivilized known world. You can transmit money from Philadelphia to any part of the civilized world, surely, securely, quickly and easily. We can read books, either in foreign languages—if we know them—or in translations, books which put us in direct communication with the thoughts and feelings of distant peoples. Many of us have friendships which bind us closely to members of various nations of the world. Those who think upon these things are sometimes apt to exaggerate the actual achievements of internationalism, and they are brought up suddenly with a sense of shock against the hard political barriers which still stand in the way of free communication of nations: barriers which thrust back our thoughts and feelings on to the conception of hard, separate and antagonistic national entities. There are many who, when the relations between nations are brought up as a subject of thought, immediately put themselves in a position of competition or antagonism. Nations seem to them natural competitors and not coöperators. In this spirit we are all of us at times almost instinctively apt to interpret some great event that has happened—the success of the Japanese, the national revolution in Russia, the Anglo-French entente, the digging of the Panama canal—we are exceedingly apt to consider how these things will affect the strength of particular nations, and their grouping for competitive purposes, in commerce and in military matters. Education, the meagre and unintelligent way in which history is taught to us, not merely in the schools but in common contact of life, is largely responsible for this idea of nations as hard, separate unities, and the phrases which have caught upon our minds in the schools, phrases like "the balance of power," "the concert of Europe" (a concert which is always conceived, not in terms of unison, but rather antagonism and opposition), such terms as these are those that unhappily express the relations between nations. When we are discussing freely the possibility of the settlement of disputes between nations by arbitration, we are still met by the dominant theory that arbitration can only deal with certain sorts of issues, and that we must reserve all those affecting the honor and the vital interests of nations from any such pacific settlement by a court of international justice; we must still retain for these important issues the right to determine our own cause for ourselves. The idea of international relations which underlies this view is that of a poise, balance, or adjustment. I will ask you to distrust such mechanical analogies as applies to social affairs. The history of modern nations has disclosed two forms in which this balance of interests is conceived; one of them is known in England and presumably over the civilized world as associated with the ideas of Richard Cobden. Cobden and his friends primarily conceived nations as bound together by the play of purely commercial interests. If we could have free trade established between the different parts of the world, then the material business interests of these different parts would bind togther the world so closely and so quickly that it would be impossible for war to be maintained in the future. The society of nations was represented by this dream as a joint stock company, determined in its relations and in its constitution by considerations of purely utilitarian harmony, each seeking to get for itself the largest quantity of material wealth. Those who see to-day that the fiercest struggles between members of different nations are for the markets of the world smile scornfully on this dream of Richard Cobden. What Cobden and his friends failed to take account of was the continued power of certain classes of interests within the nation, as distinguished from the national interests conceived as a whole—the power of certain people to misrepresent the people. The identity of commercial interests which he saw between different nations is real and substantial, and commerce might have been made the great peacemaker if the antagonism of groups within the nations had not been so powerful as to override the community of interests between peoples. Cobden, of course, and his friends, and the spirit of his time, made overmuch of commerce. We now understand that nations, like individuals, "cannot live by bread alone," but by every sound feeling that comes forth from the heart of humanity.

But there has grown up and thrives in modern times a new conception which is perhaps more fatal than this former. Our new imperalists to-day have also their dream. That dream is that the world is destined by absorption on the part of the stronger nations to pass into a smaller number of vast estates, so large and so strong that they will find it necessary to come into closer union with one another, because the shock of arms and the waste of competition will prove too disastrous. When the lions have swallowed up all the lambs, then with glutted appetites a certain torpor will come, and from that torpor they predict a world peace. The nations grown so big, so rich, so strong, will fear to oppose one another in mortal combat, so they will be driven to come to terms; a few gigantic empires dividing the earth between them, conterminous with one another, powerful, definite and rich, will form a new sort of equilibrium of forces—fear, not gain, and not love, is designated as the ultimate peacemaker. But this equilibrium of

mutual fear is as far from true attainment as the Cobdenite
dream—perhaps it is farther, if we look upon the actual condition of the world to-day. It is not true that the whole
world has been absorbed or digested by a few great nations, or
is on the point of being so digested. The seven great western
powers of the world have already before them the absorption
and the assimilation of nearly half the world which remains
undivided. Even in Europe itself we have huge tracts of territory, the Turkish empire, and to that we must now add the
great Russian empire, broken up, as it now seems, or breaking up, into new fragments. Even in Europe itself, there
seems to be an enormous task to be achieved before we can
attain anything that could be called a stable equilibrium of
powers, or any confederation of European States. In Asia
there are the great countries of China, Turkestan, Persia,
Afghanistan and Arabia, and all the vague country known as
Asia Minor. In Africa, besides the existence of the four
independent states, there are huge tracts in the interior of
Africa which are only nominally partitioned[1] among the
civilized nations of the world. In America I need only mention
that medley of weak republics in South America. These parts
of the world's surface, you will say, are loosely ear-marked by
the civilized nations as "buffer states," "spheres of influence"
or "spheres of interest," or some other in that sliding scale of
aggrandizing terms is applied to them, marking them out for
future absorption by one or other of their great civilized
neighbors. But the notion that this is the beginning of rapid
and final assimilation of the lower nations of the world is quite
unwarranted in fact, and we are far too hasty in our own gen-
eralizations to the effect that the future belongs to the great
empires. The movement for the development of great empires
has gone on very rapidly in recent times, but we have no assure-
ment that the true stability of national life will be maintained
in these great, gigantic federations of states. Moreover, mos
of the territory which has been acquired by the civilized nations
within the last thirty years is held very slightly and upon a
most precarious tenure. The dream of a single empire in the
future, or of a stable equilibrium of a few empires, dividing

among them the power of the world, and existing in amicable relations with one another, proceeding upon the line of national self-development purely, is to my mind less warranted than even the dream of Cobden.

We may ask then, is there no hope for a sound settlement of international differences and relations? Are nations inherently and eternally separate and hostile, forming among themselves temporary alliances for offense and defense, establishing balances of power, liable always to be upset by some new shift of events. It is strange how a fallacy which has been long discredited for human nature in the individual survives when we regard human nature in the nation. The doctrine associated with the philosopher Thomas Hobbes, the view that individuals existed originally in what he called a state of nature, where each man was at war with his fellows, and that individuals passed from this condition of hostility by means of what he called the social contract, agreeing with one another by means of mutual concessions to secure the self-interest of one another, has been repudiated by all modern thinkers as giving a wrong analysis of human nature, and as being a false account of the actual origin of society. It has been well and ably pointed out by modern thinkers that man, as far as we know him in history, is not a being purely absorbed in his own self-defense and individual interests, that the social character of man is part of his nature, and therefore there is a natural origin of human society from the beginning not explained as an artificial arrangement of individual self-interests. We are sure that there never was such an individual as Hobbes and his friends pictured; that theory ignores the essentially social nature of man. History shows man in the early stages of society, nay, and animals before the stage of humanity was reached, to be gregarious and sociable, to be concerned, not merely with their own interests, but with the interests of one another; the rudiments of the highest forms of modern society are found in the lowest forms of family life; and we now trace the development of societies and of human history as a struggle for life in which the coöperative factors of human life were more important than the competitive factors, a truth which

Prince Kropotkin so powerfully expresses in his book "Mutual Aid," pointing out that the notable factor in the doctrine of biological evolution is the fact that the tribe or group or nation grows more by social and coöperative power on the part of its individual members than by anything that can be called purely individual fitness and force. We have discarded the notion of pure selfishness as a basis of development. Beyond the limits of the nation, however, this hide-bound individualism is still maintained. When we regard the society of nations, nations viewed in their relations with one another, we still say they have no natural feelings for one another, they have no instincts of mutual aid. It is a strange assumption underlying this view—the assumption that the social feelings of individual men cannot pass the limits of nationality. In other words, we refuse to entertain, in any real sense, the conception of a society of nations in which the separate nations are related to one another by similar moral and psychical ties to those which we recognize within the limits of the nation. There can be, we think, no society of nations, because there is no real sociality among nations. There is no human need in one nation of the coöperation of other nations. Some sociologists in this country and others have attempted to insist upon this doctrine that the social nature of man is virtually confined to our relations within the nation, that outside the nation we have a condition of relations and an ethics which must be entirely separate from those within the national group. Among individuals in the nation the cruder forms of conflict are put down, the coöperative factor is recognized as a source of strength, the struggle, we recognize, is less a struggle for life itself, more a struggle to secure control of the environment. But all this, we say, is not applicable to the struggle between nations. The most urgent need for us, I think, is to break down this theory and this feeling about the separateness of so-called independent nations. For this hard-shell nationalism is false in the same way and to the same degree as the hard-shell individualism of the older times. The nature of a nation is not such as these people represent it, the contention that nations have no duties one to another of the same kind and in the same degree as the duties between members of a nation is false. The instinct for internationalism is just the same within the nation as the instinct for society within the individual. It weaves, as we now see if we look clearly upon the events of to-day, a subtle network of institutions which transcend the nationality.

I cannot take time to dwell upon this subject, but you will find, if you consider this subject closely, that although the political relations between nations to-day are slight, the commercial and the scientific relations between nations in various spheres of action are growing closer and more constant all the time, and that is a true basis of internationalism to which political relations will have to adjust themselves. Political forms are already growing up to support and to express this actual union of interest and sympathy which has already formed between the members of different nations. So nations coming gradually to recognize those rights and duties which actually exist, must come by degrees to substitute a settlement of differences by arbitration for settlement by force of arms.

Yet how slow this idea is to gain assent may be illustrated by the views of one of our great ethical teachers in England of recent years, the late Prof. Ritchie: "There is only one way in which war between independent nations can be prevented, and that is by the nations ceasing to be independent." Now that is a most fallacious way of presenting the idea of internationalism. We do not insist that liberty or the true independence of nations shall be curtailed. A nation no more loses its freedom and liberty by entering into organic relations with other nations than the individual does by entering into organic relations with his fellow-citizens. We understand that a properly established state in a civilized community is engaged in enlarging the liberty of its members, and what is true of the individual is equally true for nations. There is no loss of nationality in entering into just organic relations. By giving up the right of individual war, by abandoning the right to fight duels or to murder a person who offends him in a society, a citizen does not lose his freedom in any true sense. We recognize that the true liberty of the individual gains precisely by the establishment of this just social order in the state, and so it is in the establishment of an international state. The freedom of nationality, so far from being impaired, is actually fed and ripened by the establishment of international relations upon a just basis. The antagonism between nations will disappear just so far as we establish this new relation, and for its establishment one thing is necessary. The apparent oppositions of interest between nations, I repeat, are not oppositions between the interests of the people conceived as a whole; they are oppositions of class interests within the nation. The interests of America and Great Britain and France and Germany are common. The interests between certain groups of manufacturers or traders or politicians or financiers may be antagonistic at certain times within those groups, and those antagonisms, usurping the names of national interest, impose themselves as directors of the course of history; that is the actual difficulty with which we are confronted in desiring the establishment of a basis of effective internationalism. It is not a new story. The great German philosopher Kant recognized it very clearly a century and a half ago, when he wrote thus: "For if fortune ordains that a powerful and enlightened people should form a republic, which by its very nature is inclined to perpetuate peace, this would serve as a centre of federal union for other states to join, and thus secure conditions of freedom among the states." In accordance with the idea of the law of nations, gradually, through different unions of this kind, federation would extend further and further. That is to say, the conception of a real republic, by which is meant an effective democracy, is essential to the achievement of peaceable relations between the nations of the world; not of course the mere form of a republic, not a form in which the power of the people is usurped by bosses and formally registered by the vote of the people, but a real republic in which the people themselves, the several units, express themselves with freedom and equality in the determination of their own affairs. If only we get republics of that order, and not till then, shall we be able securely and effectively to achieve this great condition of a society of nations animated by the true spirit of humanity.   J. A. HOBSON.

LONDON.

Article 6

South Africa as an Imperial Asset

By J. A. Hobson

THOSE who ten years ago insisted with so much assurance upon the inevitability of war in South Africa, failed to recognise that the sequel of the war was equally inevitable. That the most redoubtable Boer Generals, who eight years ago were in the field against our troops, should now be in London imposing on the British Government the terms of a national Constitution which will make them and their allies in the Cape the rulers of a virtually independent South Africa is, indeed, one of the brightest humours of modern history. The irony gets a broader touch of humour when Generals Smuts and Hertzog are gravely summoned to advise in the defence of the Empire. The general view of the British public towards this outcome is one of mingled amazement and goodwill. This popular sentiment is in part penitence for a half-recognised misdeed, in part pride in our magnanimity, and in part a curious feeling that union has justified the war. In fact, there are not wanting persons who believe not merely that there would have been no union without the war, but that the sole motive of the war was to bring about the union. But those who fasten their eyes on the abiding factors in the history of South Africa know that, war or no war, the achievement of political union between the free self-governing States lay in the early future as a settled fact. Even before the spread of railways, and the new direction thus given to the course of trade, the issue was assured. For though the premature endeavour of British statesmen to force the pace by pressure from without in 1878, and again by conspiring with financial politicians on the spot in 1895, paralysed for a time the internal forces working for union, these latter had too much vitality to suffer more than a brief check. Even had there been no war, the needs of union were ripening so fast that it is quite likely that consummation might have been achieved as early, though the Dutch supremacy which it embodies and assures would have been less conspicuous and the form of the union would probably have been less closely knit. The absence of strong national barriers, save in the case of Natal, the similarity of racial, industrial, political and social conditions throughout the country, the free interchange for purposes of business and of settlement between the white inhabitants of the several States, the community of interest in customs, transport, education, sanitation, finance and above all else, in native policy, were forces whose acceleration and direction were constant and uniform. The devastation of the war, with its fearful aftermath of poverty and universal distress, may, indeed, have precipitated action in its final stage. Adversity makes strange bedfellows and perhaps rendered easier that co-operation of Boers with Randlords, Bondmen with Progressives, which has been so interesting a feature in the making of the Constitution. One thing is certain. It welded into a passionate spirit of unity and fixed resolve that somewhat torpid and precarious sympathy between the Dutch of the Colony and of the two erstwhile Republics, which hitherto had failed to keep them to any lasting co-operation. So defective, indeed, was this sympathy before the war that within a single decade the members of a race alleged to be possessed by the single passion to drive the British into the sea were several times upon the very verge of an armed struggle among themselves over some question of trade or of right of way. The war has not made the Union, but it has made Dutch mastery within the Union. To some it seems that the present control of the Dutch in three of the four provinces and so in the Union is the mere turn of the scales in the changing fortunes of popular election. But I feel sure that the keen-witted and loyal statesmen, who ten years ago defeated our armies and to-day rule our South African colonies, gauge the situation more truly. Our national sentimentalism befogs our vision. It delights us to imagine that at the close of a bloody and prolonged struggle, in which we wore down resistance by sheer dint of numbers, Briton and Boer should grasp hands of friendship, mutual respect warming into affection, every past unpleasantness at once forgotten, and all determined to live together happily for ever afterwards. A nice propriety of loyal speech in some of the Boer leaders may, indeed, be adduced in support of this romantic view of history. But it is foolish for those who wish to understand and estimate the future of the country where such bitter deeds were done to accept at their face value these polite assurances of oblivion. Loyalty under a flag which shall allow them perfect liberty to use their superior solidarity and persistency in shaping the destiny of the country they regard as peculiarly theirs, it is, indeed, reasonable to expect, but forgetfulness of the violence of the conquest, of the thousands of children whose death by disease and starvation in the concentration camps blackens almost every family record in the two new colonies, such amnesty is not bought by the new glory of entering an Empire upon which the sun never sets, with its alien heritage of history.

I do not dwell upon this necessary imperfection of Imperial sympathy to suggest that it is likely to affect the practical relations between the South African Union and Great Britain. When the Peace of Vereiniging was made, the future of South Africa was marked out quite irrespective of the shifts of party power either in that country or in this. If Lord Milner had looked before he leaped ten years ago he would have recognised that the surest way to render certain for the future that "dominion of Africanderdom" which he hated, was to convert the two Republics by force into two self-governing British Colonies. For, even if the Government which had made the war had kept the reins of office afterwards, with Lord Milner as their authoritative adviser, the utmost they could have achieved would have been a postponement of complete self-government for a few years, accompanied with jerrymandering of constituencies designed to favour British voters ; a policy which might have goaded the Boers to political reprisals when they entered on the full colonial status which the first entry of a Liberal Government in England must have secured to them, but which could have had no abiding influence upon the further course of events.

But though it is probable that the greater stability and the more prolific character of the Dutch will make them the chief formative stock in the amalgam of the new South African nation, while the persistence of the Taal and of the Dutch-Roman law will maintain strongly distinctive features in this section of our Empire, the trend of national development will not differ materially from that of Canada or Australia, so far as its relations towards Great Britain and her sister nations in the Empire are concerned. How are these relations shaping ? Among those who accept as final the sharp distinction which has hitherto been drawn between those white colonies ripe or ripening for self-government and the unfree remainder of our Empire, it is natural that the achievement of South African Union should bring this question into new prominence. For to Mr. Chamberlain, as twenty years before to Lord Carnarvon, this union, however desirable upon its own account, had its chief significance as a step towards a larger federation, or other reconstitution of the self-governing sections of the British Empire. Group federation was to be followed by Imperial Federation. The former process is now nearly complete in the Canadian Dominion, the

SOUTH AFRICA AS AN IMPERIAL ASSET

Australian Commonwealth, and the South African Union. Whether New Zealand elects still to stand alone, or, as is not unlikely, is drawn into an Australasian Union by the supreme need of a strong Pacific policy, is a question of no present urgency. Other fragments still remain for inevitable absorption, Newfoundland in Canada, Rhodesia in the South African Union. But does this grouping of adjoining colonies into nations evidently favour the ideal of a close-linked British Empire of which Imperialists have dreamed?

Does the smaller centralising process imply the larger one? The general trend of colonial history during the last three-quarters of a century supports no such implication. As each colony has grown in population, wealth, and enterprise it has persistently asserted larger rights of independent government which the Mother Country has, sometimes willingly, sometimes reluctantly, conceded : each colony values among its most prized traditions the successful resistance to some acts of interference on the part of the Imperial Government which it has deemed injurious to its vital interests or offensive to its sense of dignity, some endeavour to restrict its territorial growth, to force upon it undesirable immigrants, to coerce its commercial liberty. But in general the lesson of the colonies contained in the American Revolution has sufficed to teach us acquiescence in the continuous assertion of larger independence. The actual bonds, alike political and commercial, between the several colonies and the Mother Country have been growing every decade weaker, in spite of the greater physical accessibility which the steamer and the telegraph have brought, and in spite of the great machinery of modern investment which every colony has used so freely to draw capital from Great Britain for her own developement. Nor is it without significance that the oldest and the nearest colonies, and those which federated first among themselves, have gone furthest in the practical assertion of an independence which now leaves Imperial control and obligations well-nigh divested of all corresponding rights even in issues of foreign policy.

When the power to place protective tariffs on our goods and to make their own commercial treaties with foreign countries was once conceded, it needed no undue insistence upon the economic interpretation of history to see that a continual evolution both of commercial and of political self-sufficiency must follow. As each colony fell into federation with its neighbours, this spirit and this practice of autonomy naturally grew, and the four nations now forming part of our overseas empire are firmer in their confident self-sufficiency than ever were the constituent colonies. Those British Imperialists who, with the events of the last few years before their eyes, still imagine a closer Imperial federation in any shape or form practicable, are merely the dupes of Kiplingesque sentimentalism.

It is true that these Colonies sent gallant troops (at our expense) to our assistance in the Boer War, and that for purposes of Imperial defence the British Flag may remain a real asset, though, as the recent Conference will clearly show, the same spirit of separatism exhibited in politics and in commerce demands that even in defence, National shall always take precedence of Imperial interests. Though in each colony aspiring politicians have been found to fan Imperialist sentiment to a glow and to utilise the heat for electoral purposes or for personal glory, these bursts of effervescent feeling, however genuine while they last, cannot be taken as serious factors in the shaping of their national policy. The pride in the British connection may bring Canadian, Australian and South African statesmen to toy with suggestions of political or commercial federation on decorative occasions such as Imperial Conferences : it may even evoke some sentimental dole of preference in a colonial tariff, or some eleemosynary contribution towards a British fleet, but it will not lead the people of these countries on this ground to abate one jot or one tittle of their fixed determination to go their own way, to develope their own natural resources for their own sole advantage, and to be guided in all important acts of policy by purely National, as distinct from Imperial, objects. The very notion that Canada, Australia, New Zealand, or South Africa will even consider the advisability of entering a close political union, through the formation of some Imperial Council, which, whether vested with legislative powers or not, could only act by restricting liberties hitherto enjoyed by each colonial unit, is acknowledged to be chimerical by most of those who in the nineties were enamoured of the project.

Mr. Chamberlain soon saw that the front-door of political federation was shut, bolted and barred. He thereupon sought the tradesman's entrance, claiming to knit the colonies and the Mother Country into an indissoluble union by means of a set of preferences which he hoped might eventually give free trade within the Empire. We now perceive that the appeal to community of trading interests is as futile as was the earlier appeal, and for the same reason. Each of our offspring nations is determined to consult its own interests, and it finds that these interests are opposed to any commercial union. This for two reasons : first, because such commercial union to be valid must imply some subordination of its own immediate interests to the co-operative trading ends of the Empire, and to such restraint it will not submit ; secondly, because experience, as registered in trade statistics, shows that its commercial interests lie more in the developement of profitable trade relations with foreign countries than in British or intra-Imperial trade. The recent commercial history of Canada and Australia proves that each nation has made up its mind to utilise its tariff system, first for its own industrial developement, secondly, for its own financial needs. If British preference is retained at all, it can afford no substantial gain and no considerable bond, for British import trade must neither compete with colonial industries nor hamper the colony in negotiating special trade agreements with foreign countries. A detailed examination of Canadian preference proves how flimsy is this bond of union.

It remains for the future to show whether Imperial defence can draw the Empire nearer together, or whether it also will yield to the disintegrating forces. One thing, however, is certain. If the Colonial Office is used again as it was used by Mr. Chamberlain to procure offers of colonial aid, if British Governments, Unionist or Liberal, angle for colonial gift-ships by scare-cables with crooked phrases, all that is generous and genuine in the colonial concern for the old Motherland will perish. No one can have consorted freely with colonial visitors this summer without noting the tone of surprised contempt for the " jumpy " nerves evinced during the months of the German panic. The impudent perversion of the Imperial Press Conference to the same single purpose provoked significant protests from leading colonial journalists whose indignation was aroused at the materialistic interpretation given by British statesmen to Imperial unity. Just as participation in the Boer War opened the eyes of Canadian and Australian volunteers to the military weakness of England, so this eager pleading for Imperial defence rouses reflections upon the character of the Empire, the risks it involves for the self-governing nations, and the unequal influence which they will exercise in determining Imperial policy. It might well appear a profitable and glorious task to co-operate in the protection of a " free, tolerant, unaggressive " Empire. But it is not equally glorious or profitable for a free-born Canadian or New Zealander to enter a confederation under which a necessarily dominant partner can claim his blood and money to help hold down India, to quell some struggle for liberty in Egypt, or to procure some further step in tropical aggrandisement at the bidding of some mining or rubber syndicate. In other words, it is our huge, "unfree, intolerant, aggressive" Empire which may well give pause to our self-governing colonies when invited to enter a close unity of Imperial defence. For this Empire is no real concern of theirs, they have nothing in common with its modes of autocratic government, they are unwilling even to admit its " British subjects " on to their shores. Why then should they feign enthusiasm for an Imperial defence mainly directed to maintain and enlarge this unfree Empire by quarrels to which they are no willing parties, in which no true interests of theirs will be involved, but in which they may be called upon to squander their resources and even risk their independence.

Though the full logic of the situation may not yet be manifest, we may be sure that it is a sound prophetic instinct which makes colonial statesmen so reluctant to commit their countries to any of those schemes of close central control which our home-made Imperialists have been so anxious to bind upon them. Nothing is more significant than the determined way in which the colonies, Canada leading, are urging the conditions of their participation in Imperial defence, viz., the priority of Colonial to Imperial defence with all its necessary limitations in Imperial strategy, and the retention of the *personnel* of the command in the hands of the Colonial Government.

Of the real meaning of this movement there can be no doubt. As in political self-government and in commerce, each colonial group has long established a virtually complete autonomy, so now it is proposed to take over the duty and the right of its armed defence from the Mother Country. As soon as the so-called " Imperial Defence " is consummated, there will be no Imperial troops or ships in the "free" colonies, but only national troops and national ships. Whatever language is used to describe this new movement of Imperial defence it is virtually one more step towards complete national independence on the part of the colonies. For not only will the consciousness of the assumption of this task of self-defence feed with new vigour the spirit of nationality, it will entail the further power of full control over foreign relations. This has already been virtually admitted in the case of Canada, now entitled to a determinant voice in all treaties or other engagements in which her interests are especially involved. The extension of this right to the other colonial nations may be taken as a matter of course. Home rule in national defence thus established reduces the Imperial connection to its thinnest terms.

To speculators upon the larger problems of history it will be a particularly interesting and delicate consideration whether our colonial nations will best consult their safety and their liberty in the future by remaining formal members of the Empire, sharing both the risks and the resources of this association, or by taking their destinies entirely into their own hands, forming their own alliances, and meeting out of their own resources the rarer risks which might attend such severance.

But the formation of the South African Union emphasises in another way the instability of the British Empire. "I believe this Government," said Abraham Lincoln, "cannot endure permanently half slave, half free." Equally true is it that no abiding unity can be found for an Empire half autocratic and half self-governing. One force of dissolution we have already recognised in the divorce alike of sympathy and interest between the self-governing colonies and the rest of the overseas dominions of the Crown. But the corruption of self-government itself in the case of the new nation is a perhaps more subtle sign of weakness and decay. The constitution of the South African Union is, indeed, in some respects a more satisfactory instrument of government than either that of the Canadian Dominion or of the Australian Commonwealth. In this country it has been subjected to very little criticism. Both parties appear to regard the sanction of the Imperial Parliament as an act destitute of real responsibility. It is, indeed, understood that the Colonial Office has procured some minor modifications in the South African proposals. But all effective criticism or amendment has been denied to the House of Commons by a bold and very simple form of bluff. The South African delegates, who came here to impose this Act of Union, were well aware that the denial of any real representation to civilised natives and coloured people over the greater part of the Union, the imperilling of the coloured franchise in the Cape and, in particular, the formal adoption of a colour-line for membership of the Union Assembly, would be unwelcome to the majority of the members of the most Liberal Parliament which has ever sat in Westminster. Aware that any free exercise of Imperial legislative power would amend their Act so as to secure the standard of equality formulated by Mr. Rhodes, "equal rights for all civilised men south of the Zambesi," they agreed upon the terse formula that any such amendment would "wreck the Union!" The device was well calculated to secure its end. For though it is utterly unreasonable to suppose that the South African States, each with such carefully bargained ends to gain by union, would, in fact, withdraw their sanction because the Imperial Government chose to exercise its undoubted right to secure for the majority of British subjects in South Africa the right to qualify for civilisation, the firm assertion of this peril proved enough to overbear the opposition of all save a negligible minority. It was inevitable that this should be so.

The fast confederacy of Dutch and British politicians was certain to bear down principles of Liberalism already compromised and enfeebled by acquiescence in the modes of government applied by Lord Morley and Sir Edward Grey to the subjects of our unfree Empire.

So it has come about that a government has been established in South Africa, in form resembling that of Canada, Australia and New Zealand, in substance very different. To describe as a self-governing nation the white oligarchy that has, with our connivance, fenced itself against admission of the ablest and most progressive members of races living in their midst and by general admission capable of a civilisation at least as high as that of the ordinary white wage-earner, is an outrage to political terminology. Deliberately to set out upon a new career as a civilised nation upon a definition of civilisation which takes race and colour, not individual character and attainments, as the criterion is nothing else than to sow a crop of dark and dangerous problems for the future. Such a government, such a civilisation, must fall between two stools. There is, indeed, no parallel without or within the Empire for a self-government in which five-sixths of the governed are excluded from all rights of citizenship. In other colonies where the population is mainly composed by " lower races " bureaucracy is never more than tempered by representation, and that representation is mostly free from colour-lines : such government can at least secure order, if at the cost of progress. It is conceivable (though our Empire affords no present instance) that sound order and political serenity might be attained by a white oligarchy which kept in economic servitude the lower races of inhabitants, barred them from skilled industries, from any large participation in modern city life, and from religious and intellectual instruction of any kind. This was virtually the old Boer policy, though adopted as readily by British settlers on the land ; it was absolutely successful. But it is not comformable to-day either to the conditions or the sentiments of the more progressive white citizens of South Africa, even in Natal. There is no intention to refuse all technical and intellectual education to Zulus, Fingos, and other natives capable of profiting by it ; much of the hard work which Europeans will continue to require and will refuse to do themselves involves and evokes knowledge, intelligence, and a sense of personal responsibility. Not even the most carefully sophisticated Christianity,

furnished by " kept " white missionaries, can prevent the democratic doctrines of the New Testament from doing this revolutionary work.

To take away the political liberties enjoyed for a third of a
century in Cape Colony would prove too dangerous : to leave
them will be to set a continuously growing ferment at work
throughout the length and breadth of the Union. For there are
very deep and very real native grievances. In the Transvaal and
Orange River Colony the elementary freedom of movement
from one place to another is denied, the right of buying and
holding land is denied : whenever in South Africa a dispute arises
between a white and a coloured man it is tried in a white man's
court, by white man's justice. Indeed it is needless to labour
such an issue : political rights are everywhere the indispensable
condition of civil rights, and without them can be no security of
life, liberty and property for an " inferior " race or class.

I am well aware that public opinion is very unenlightened
among the bulk of the white population of South Africa. Many
of the political leaders confess themselves favourable to a carefully restricted native franchise, but insist that " the people will
not have it." But I cannot help feeling that if these statesmen had taken a little more time to forecast the troubles which are
certain to arise from an essentially inconsistent native policy, such
as I have here described, they would have thrown the full weight
of their personal authority, never likely to be greater than now,
against the popular prejudice, and have welcomed the aid of our
Liberal Government to support a Constitution free from this
stain of colour. There can be no enduring peace, no steady progress and prosperity in a South Africa where the vast bulk of the
work of industry is done by men who are denied all opportunity
to participate, proportionately to their proved capacity, in the
government of the country which is morally theirs, in the sense
that they are genuinely interested in it and have put their
personal effort into its developement.

At the best such a South African Union as is now established
will be a close replica not of Canada, but of the Southern States
of the American Commonwealth, where the races subsist side by
side in the same land in no organic spiritual contact with one
another, each race suffering the moral, intellectual and industrial
penalty of this disunion. As the recent spread of education and
of skilled industry among the negroes of these Southern States
has only served to develope and aggravate the situation, so it will
be in South Africa. There, as in the Southern States, the black
population grows at least as fast as the white, it cannot be ex-

pelled or put into reserves because it is required for white men's wants, it cannot be permanently kept in ignorance, and knowledge means not only power but the demand for rights and a rising discontent at their denial.

The higher mental calibre and capacity of many of the Bantu peoples and the presence of considerable numbers of unintelligent Asiatics will be likely to ripen in South Africa even more rapidly than in the Southern States this sense of wrong and this demand for justice. This claim is misunderstood when it is resolved into a race question. Though the form of the exclusion gives it that aspect, it is not at root a race question but a question of personality. The Zulu, the Indian, who is denied a voice in his country, does not say, " Give me a vote because a Zulu, or an Indian, is as good as a white man." He says, " Give me a vote because by any reasonable test of manhood you lay down—work, knowledge, personal character, even property—I am as fit a man to serve the State as others whom you admit." Unless and until the sentiments of the white peoples in South Africa can be adjusted to the acceptance of this humane and just view of a State, one which can only operate by raising the average standard of citizenship, its destiny will move upon an unstable axis, and it will remain a source, not of strength, but of weakness to the group of self-governing nationalities to which it falsely claims to belong.

Article 7

THE GENERAL ELECTION: A SOCIOLOGICAL INTERPRETATION.*

It is impossible for me, perhaps for anyone else, to perform in a really satisfactory manner the task which I have undertaken to-night. If, as has been said, prophecy is the most gratuitous form of human error, interpretation of current politics may be conceded the second place. For the ideal interpreter is himself a contradiction in terms. Interpretation is impossible without a sympathetic understanding, and a sympathy directed with entire impartiality and, what is more, capable of convincing others of that impartiality, is not attainable. For what sort of a citizen would he be, who in the present current of public affairs, could guarantee to himself or to others this complete impartiality? An intelligent foreigner might indeed set forth the measurable facts of the subject without bias, but he could hardly give them the meaning and the valuation essential to the process of interpretation.

I shall not pretend the impossible. Though my treatment will be as 'sociological' as I can make it, the fact that I entertain certain political opinions implies, even in selection and ordering of material, still more in valuation and interpretation, a measure of bias for which each member of my audience must make his own allowance. I shall be content·if I can keep this bias within bounds and fairly constant in direction and intensity. For then I shall afford to those who see events with different eyes the best conditions for making an intelligible adjustment for themselves.

In laying before you what appear to me to be the chief measurable facts disclosed by the result of the general election, I must ask you further to remember that time compels a very rigorous economy of selection. Much relevant and interesting matter must be omitted from our survey.

The election results must be considered in the first place as disclosing two facts: first, the present judgment of the electorate upon a set of issues forming the substance of two, or in some cases three, policies, and recommended by the prestige of party names and leaders; second, the change that has taken place in the electoral preference since the election of four years ago qualified by some eighty bye-elections. For our purpose it is best to pay most attention to analysis and interpretation of the present judgment; for, if we hold the electoral choice to be directed at least as much by

* A Paper read before the Sociological Society, February 22, 1910.

consideration of policy as of party allegiance, we shall recognise that the shift of important issues since 1906 has been so considerable as to invalidate to an unknown extent an attempt to interpret the swing of the pendulum in any close relation to particular issues.

For obvious convenience I shall in most of my account omit Ireland, confining myself to the election in Great Britain. Some of the few figures I present will be merely approximate, partly because exact figures are not always attainable, partly because round figures are more easily comprehended and do no harm where no argument depends on their exactness.

Taking first the General Election as a Plebiscite, and counting Liberal and Labour votes together, as we are justified in doing from their close agreement on the dominant issues, we reach the following result for Great Britain :—

Liberal and Labour.	Unionist.	Majority.
3,185,250	2,904,001	281,249

a majority amounting to about 4¾ per cent. This plebiscite is of course very differently proportioned in relation to the different groups of constituencies. In London the Unionist majority amounted to about 6¾ per cent.: in the English boroughs the Liberal majority was about 4 per cent., in the English counties about ½ per cent. In Wales the Liberal vote was considerably more than double the Unionist vote (206,288 to 97,126): in Scotland the majority was nearly 20 per cent.

It will be evident from consideration of this result that, as usual, the numbers of members of the parties elected bear no just relation to the aggregate party vote.

If an equal value were secured for every vote, the majority for the Liberal and Labour parties in Great Britain would be, not 63, the actual number, but 27. The operation of our electoral machinery, as is well recognised, tends to favour the stronger party, giving it a majority in excess of its proportionate majority of votes. This excess, though considerable, is, however, far smaller than in most recent elections, as the following figures show :—

	Vote Majorities.		
	1895	1900	1906	1910
Great Britain	U. 310,632	 322,974	L. 636,418	L. 281,249
Maj. in Seats	U. 213	U. 195	L. 289	L. 63

In regarding the election as a measure of public opinion, it would, however, be necessary to exclude plural voting. This introduces a considerable element of conjecture into our arithmetic. The number of out-voters is not known. It is often roughly estimated, upon what evidence I know not, at half a million, or about 1 in 13 of the votes cast. If this is even approximately true, it evidently makes a considerable readjustment necessary in estimating the election as a plebiscite. For no one will contend that these outvotes are equally apportioned between the two parties. In the recent election it is not unreasonable to believe that four out of five were cast for the Unionist party. This estimate is defended by urging that plural voting is virtually confined to men of property, the overwhelming majority of whom, especially in the South of England where outvoters chiefly dwell, vote conservative. If half a million of such votes were actually cast and four out of five went to a Unionist, this would be equivalent to a weighting of the Unionist poll by an additional 10 per cent. of votes. Or, putting the matter in another way, the abolition of the plural voting at this election would have doubled the actual majority of Liberal votes in Great Britain, raising the majority of Liberal and Labour members, under a system of one vote one value, to a figure a little below the 63 which is their actual majority.

It is now time to consider the geographical and economic distribution of political opinion as indicated by party victories in the election. First, we are confronted by that remarkable contrast of North and South which first strikes the eye on glancing at the electoral map. A line drawn across Great Britain along the Mersey and the Trent shows an overwhelming majority of Liberal and Labour seats in the northern section, an almost equally overwhelming majority of Unionist seats in the southern section, if Wales be left out of the account. This geographical generalisation, however, requires important qualifications. The uniformity of the Unionist South is broken by substantial patches of Liberalism in the industrial part of the Metropolis, in Cornwall and Devon, and in Norfolk and Lincolnshire. Upon the other hand Unionism makes two considerable encroachments upon the Liberal North, one along the sea-coast constituencies East and West, another in a slanting wedge working through Staffordshire and Cheshire towards a point in North Lancashire. The predominance of Unionism throughout the coast constituencies is very marked, amounting in the south to an almost complete possession. The general contrast of North and South is sharpened by the fact that the further North you go the greater the compactness and the uniformity of Liberalism, while Conservatism becomes correspondingly more intense the further South you go.

The list of party gains which marks most forcibly the change of political opinion since 1906 gives striking testimony to the same general truth, showing that the Liberalism of the North is virtually unmoved, during a period when the South has undergone a profound change. For, of the 117 seats gained by Unionists in

England, 13 only stand above the line of Trent and Mersey, while 9 Liberal and Labour gains above that line reduce the net Unionist gain in the Northern Counties to 4. In Scotland the net Unionist gain was none, five seats being won by them and five lost.

A truer electoral map, which indicated by a deepening of the representative colours the size or proportion of the majority by which each seat was held, would upon the whole enforce still further the contrast of North and South, showing proportionate Liberal majorities which grew larger as you went further North, Unionist majorities largest in the most Southern Counties. The special case of the Birmingham sphere of influence would, however, qualify the operation of this general rule.

Before turning to the interpretation of these broad results I ought to remind you that the proportion of the distribution of seats in North and South respectively gives of necessity a very exaggerated notion of the distribution of political opinion. So long as there is no provision for the proportionate representation of minorities this is inevitable. The effect is to induce a belief that the North is more Liberal, the South more Conservative than is actually the case. Even in Lancashire where the Liberals claim a signal victory it is asserted by the *National Review* that nearly 45 per cent. of the votes recorded were cast for Tariff Reform.

Now, taking this geographical distribution of parties as indicated by the electoral results, we can easily apply some general principles of economic criticism. North and South correspond with certain economic distinctions. The great productive industries of manufacture and of mining are almost entirely Northern, while the South is more agricultural, its manufactures are small and less highly organised, and it contains a large number of pleasure resorts and residential towns and villages.

The statement that industrial Britain is Liberal, rural and residential Britain Conservative, is substantially accurate. It may be tested variously. London itself may be cited as a witness. Indeed the geographical distribution of electoral results in the Metropolis is the most striking corroboration of the economic interpretation of the larger contrast between North and South. For in London, East and West correspond economically with the division of North and South in the country taken as a whole, and, as a glance at the map will show, the East is entirely Liberal, the West entirely Unionist, in each case with the one exception which saves the appearance of unnatural exactitude. But when we turn from London, whose industrial conditions are unique, to the great manufacturing towns of the Midlands and the North, we find an overwhelming preponderance of Liberal seats. Even the exceptions form the rule, for Birmingham, Liverpool, Wolverhampton, Nottingham, Preston, Sunderland, are all susceptible of easy explanations based upon the special conditions of employment or of unemployment, or upon the chance of a three-cornered contest. Every other great industrial city in the country has returned a majority of Liberal members, or of Liberal votes, while the dominance of Liberalism north of the Tweed carried even the great residential capital of Scotland.

Where industrialism is most highly organised and most concentrated, upon the great coalfields of Lancashire and Yorkshire, Derbyshire, Northumberland and Durham, not to mention South Wales, the greatest intensity of Liberalism and Labourism prevails. The textile, machine-making and mining constituencies yielded almost universally the largest Liberal majorities, infecting with their views even most of the semi-agricultural constituencies in their near neighbourhood. The Liberal predominance in the North may be thus summarised. Scotland and North England, including Lancashire, Yorkshire, Durham, Northumberland, Cumberland, Westmorland, Derbyshire and Cheshire, send to Parliament 175 Liberal and Labour men and 54 Unionists. Hardly less concentrated is the Unionist power in the home and Southern counties. Kent, Surrey, Sussex, Hertfordshire and Huntingdon are held entire, while Middlesex and Warwickshire show only one Liberal seat. Almost every old cathedral city, with the exception of one or two important industrial centres such as Durham, York, and Norwich, nearly all the dockyard and service towns, the watering places and pleasure resorts, the county towns throughout the South, the old market towns, which return a member of bulk largely in some county constituency, cast substantial majorities for the Unionists.

Most instructive is the test of Unionist gains. With the exception of a few seats in Lancashire and Staffordshire and half a dozen of the London seats, the 117 Unionist gains in England were almost wholly composed of non-industrial towns and purely agricultural or residential county constituencies.

This tabulation will suffice to enable us to understand why the political issues set before the electorate produced such different results in North and South Britain. The three positive issues of prime importance were the Lords' Veto, the Land policy contained in or associated with the Budget, and Tariff Reform. Two other issues, though of inferior formal importance, namely, the liquor taxation and the German scare must, however, be accorded a prominent part in influencing votes, particularly in London and in the smaller older boroughs. To Home Rule, the Education Question and other older issues I do not assign wide influence in determining votes or the results of elections, except in a few special cases.

To attempt any assessment of the relative value of these issues as influencing the result of elections is of course a very hazardous proceeding. The view stated here is only to be taken as a register of the impressions gathered from conversation with active politicians, some personal observation and copious reading of the press of both parties.

The solidarity of Liberalism in the North and generally in the great industrial centres may, I think, be regarded as an endorsement of an Anti-Veto policy, Land Reform and Free Trade, with a fairly equal valuation of the three issues. The Lords and the Land probably bulked more largely as the really live issues in Scotland and the Northern English counties, where Tariff Reform propaganda has made less progress. Though Liberal candidates and leading platform speakers all over the country placed the issue of the Lords in the front of their appeal, it did not play so considerable a part off the platform, and in the Midlands and South it was certainly a subordinate influence in determining elections. The Unionist victories in the South must be attributed chiefly to a successful propaganda of Tariff Reform, mainly directed to the issue of unemployment, assisted by the unpopularity of the liquor taxes and a half-military, half-industrial fear of Germany. There are, I am aware, many other factors which deserve attention. One deserves, I think, especial mention : the failure of the Government to secure the effective administration of the Small Holdings Act was an important contributory cause to the loss of Liberal seats in the rural South.

Assuming that this general assessment of electoral issues is substantially correct, it is worth while briefly to consider the methods by which they were made effective for influencing votes. Here of course we enter the shadowy, or shady, region of the arts of electioneering. How far, and in what sense, can the verdict of the electorate be regarded as a reasoned judgment, how far was it procured by strong subconscious or irrational suggestion, how far by the mere mechanics of electioneering, how far by intimidation or sheer bribery? No man can answer such questions with confidence or any safe precision. I will, however, venture the following opinions. The abnormal fierceness of a contest in which pocket-interests bulked more largely and more clearly than at any previous election, probably evoked a certain recrudescence of those practices of bribery, treating and intimidation, which, once general, have never died out of our electioneering. In certain constituencies where traditions of corruption and servility survive, and where the conditions of work enable pressure to be brought to bear upon numbers of poor electors in precarious employment, such malpractices may have affected the result. But, making due allowance for the tendency of the defeated party to exaggerate the amount of unfair play, where some unfairness exists, I am not disposed to set down very much to the score of bribery or direct intimidation. No doubt 'moral influence,' to use a dubious phrase, which comprises respect for the known opinion of 'our betters' and a general desire to stand well with the gentry and those who can influence business or employment, counted more heavily than usual. But even then the line between such personal influence and the impersonal appeal of political issues is hard to draw. Personal or business interests everywhere help to drive home arguments or to give efficacy to emotional suggestions.

No student of electioneering is likely to underrate the part played by emotional suggestion. But it may easily be exaggerated. Even the familiar appeals to party allegiance are not merely emotional, still less merely subconscious; they contain some element of rational appeal. The figure of a Duke who asks you to 'get off his earth,' of a foreigner who has 'got your job,' or of a dissipated London corner-man who 'wants work,' are no doubt intended to impose rather than to educate opinion. But none the less they do serve to evoke reflection. Everywhere knots of men, gathering round these placards, were stimulated or provoked to reasoned controversy. I would venture to assert that there has never been an election in which reasoned discussion has been so widespread and played so large a part in determining results. Nor would I apply this only to the North, where by general consent the level of intelligence and intellectual interest among the working classes is higher than in the South.

The Tariff Reform victory in the South was obtained upon the whole by convincing the understanding of the active minds of the electorate. Although many of the facts adduced were false and most of the reasoning faulty, it was a serious attempt to present a reasoned fiscal policy, directed chiefly to prove that Protection could increase employment. Indeed the failure of Free Trade to find effective platform arguments to meet the contention entitles Protectionists fairly to claim an argumentative victory upon this head. Though political education of a formal sort has made little advance in any class, the magnitude and even the dramatic character of the new issues do much more than influence the passions; everywhere in various degrees they awaken reflection and stimulate the reasoning faculties. The result is that elections are coming gradually to depend less, not more, upon mere skill of electioneering: sound facts and right reasoning are gradually coming to possess an increased advantage over unsound facts and false reasoning. It is easier to impose true than false suggestions, for they are less likely to be 'found out' when every electorate comes to contain a leaven of intelligent and informed minds.

One other point connected with electioneering deserves mention. It is probably the case that in the South, where men of property are more numerous and are more predominantly Conservative, the mere mechanics of electioneering was used with more effect than any sort of bribery or intimidation to secure Conservative majorities. The machinery of registration, the co-operation of 'the trade' and of other outside agencies, and, in particular, the services of the motor car, probably account to a considerable extent for the increase in the Unionist poll.

Having now disposed, however imperfectly, of the main external features of the general election, let us turn once more to investigate more closely the significance of the contrast between political opinion in the North and South, in industrial and non-industrial Britain. What is the difference in character or disposition of electors which induces the cathedral and residential cities of the well-to-do, the watering places, service towns and feudal ruralism to vote for Tariff Reform and the Lords, while the manufacturing and mining centres with the more independent agricultural population of the North declare for the Budget, Land Reform and the legislative liberty of the representative House? Before suggesting an answer to this question, it is, however, right to call attention to one interesting result of the election which appears to conflict with the economic generalisation presented here. I allude of course to what is known as the Birmingham area. In this part of the Midlands a large group of definitely industrial constituencies has severed itself from the rest of industrial Britain. This severance would itself form a valuable subject of sociological enquiry. How much weight should be assigned to the extraordinary personal prestige of Mr. Chamberlain, how much to efficient operation of the political machine first made in Birmingham, how much to the fact that a large number of the trades upon which this district is dependent, are carried on in small factories or workshops which do not favour effective Trade Unionism, and are engaged in making goods which are exposed to close foreign competition, to an unusual extent? I do not possess knowledge enabling me to answer these questions : it is, however, probable that each of the considerations I suggest contributes to the result, and perhaps further allowance should be made for obscure but strong influences of local pride in adhering to a policy which has evoked so much interest and so much criticism.

But the importance of this exceptional area is not such as to destroy the validity of the general distinction between industrial North and non-industrial South.

The two Englands, to which the electoral map gives substantially accurate expression, may be described as a Producer's England and a Consumer's England, one England in which the well-to-do classes, from their numbers, wealth, leisure and influence, mould the external character of the civilisation and determine

the habits, feelings and opinions of the people, the other England
in which the structure and activities of large organised industries,
carried on by great associated masses of artisans, factory hands
and miners, are the dominating facts and forces. The Home
Counties, the numerous seaside and other residential towns, the
cathedral and university towns, and in general terms, the South,
are full of well-to-do and leisured families, whose incomes, disso-
ciated from any present exertion of their recipients, are derived
from industries conducted in the North or in some over-sea country.
A very large share, probably the major part, of the income spent
by these well-to-do residential classes in the South, is drawn from
possessions or investments of this nature. The expenditure of
these incomes calls into existence and maintains large classes of
professional men, producers and purveyors of luxuries, tradesmen,
servants and retainers, who are more or less conscious of their
dependence on the goodwill and patronage of persons 'living on
their means.' This class of 'ostentatious leisure' and 'conspicuous
waste ' is subordinated in the North to earnest industry : in the
South it directs a large proportion of the occupations, sets the
social tone, imposes valuations and opinions. This England is
primarily regarded by the dominant class as a place of residence
and a playground, in which the socially reputable sports and
functions (among which church-going, the theatre, art, and certain
mild forms of literary culture are included), may be conducted with
dignity and comfort. Most persons living in the South certainly
have to work for a living, but much of this work is closely and even
consciously directed by the will and the demands of the moneyed
class, and the prestige of the latter imposes habits, ideas and
feelings antagonistic alike to useful industry and to democracy.
Moreover (a feature related closely to the character of the expenditure) the occupations of the people in the South are principally
those of retail traders, small tenant farmers with ill-paid labourers,
and numbers of small local businesses supplying the needs of local
groups of consumers. The only great widespread industry,
building, is in structure and working widely sundered from the
great manufacturing and mining industries, and its instability
affects gravely the character of its employees. In the South there
is a great gulf fixed between the gentry and the working classes, a
class of peculiarly servile shopkeepers furnishing no proper bridge.
In the North a large proportion of the well-to-do are actively
engaged in organising and directing industry, and, more important
still, the industries support large classes of regular, well-paid,
intelligent artisans and other skilled workers. Here we reach the
chief clue to the difference of political opinion in North and South.
The Liberalism and Labourism of the North is mainly dependent
on the feelings and opinions of this upper grade of the wage-

earners, the large, new middle-class. The strength of Liberalism, as attested by the election, varies directly with the relative size and compactness of this artisan element. Almost everywhere is set against it the opinion and the vote of the great majority of the employing, the professional, the shopkeeping, the leisured classes upon the one hand, and a large proportion, usually a majority, of the casual or semi-employed manual labour, and of clerks and shop-assistants, upon the other.

Never has the cleavage been so evident before. It is organised labour against the possessing and educated classes, on the one hand, against the public house and unorganised labour, on the other. So general a statement, of course, requires qualification. With the solid mass of organised workers stands a minority of well-to-do progressives and a large various scattering of lower-grade workers. But it is substantially true that organised labour furnishes the body of the liberal electorate. It is this body that has declared most solidly and definitely for the Budget, against the Lords and against Protection. This solidarity and definiteness are so marked as to constitute a new position in our politics. Taken in conjunction with our analysis of Southern England, with its unassociated servile and ill-paid labour, it serves to bring into relief the deeper interpretation of the election. Never before have the main issues of an election been charged with so much definitely economic import. This growing pressure of economic issues is of course not now confined to this country. But recent events have accelerated the pace and imparted clearer consciousness to the movement. Imperialism, Militarism, Protection, Oligarchy, are suddenly exhibited as a dramatic company on the stage of practical politics. The party which still retains the title Conservative has delivered itself over to the powers of reaction, embodied in explicit demands for Protection and Conscription and an assertion by the hereditary House of a control over finance.

The foreign and domestic policy involved in the new front of Conservatism, aggressively reactionary in form, is best interpreted as belonging to the traditional defences to which the ruling and possessing classes instinctively resort to meet a popular attack upon their economic and social privileges. The policy of land, industrial and social reform, with its accompanying fiscal policy, to which Liberalism and Labourism are now committed, is naturally regarded by them and their intellectual and economic dependents as an attack upon property. Its advocates prefer to describe it as a readjustment of the rights of property upon a basis of greater equality of individual opportunity, with a fuller recognition of state rights in socially-erected property. However described, it involves considerable interference with, and some curtailment of, existing rights of property in land values, liquor licenses and in other sources of unearned or superfluous wealth. The organised artisans, who are the strength of the attacking or reforming forces, are not socialists or conscious idealists of any order. Though there is some logic in their aims and purposes, it is made applicable to the redress of particular concrete grievances rather than to the realisation of large general aspirations. Some patches of consciousness, dim or clear, show here and there in the general will, but for the most part the movement is instinctive. Definite problems of poverty and injustice have been stirring the minds of the working and poorer classes, and in the group-mind of the associated workmen a number of separate demands have grown into a more or less coherent policy. Freer access to land and a curbing of landlordism in town and country, public assistance against the risks and injuries of proletarian life, and a definite constructive public policy for the prevention and redress of destitution, are the strongest strains in the policy. No doubt other larger, vaguer aspirations are present, making for a fuller life, more pleasure, more knowledge, and a larger share of the wealth and leisure and other opportunities which they see provided for the few by the heavy unremitting toil of the many. Though some active minds among them form general conceptions of a socialistic state, or ride some narrower theory of a panacea, the general mind of this Liberalism is groping after near and tangible results. But the reforms they seek indisputably imply disturbances in the present private system of property and industry, and the public finance which they demand, as an adjunct, involves direct encroachments upon the possessions and incomes of the well-to-do. The power of associated labour is growing, and it is setting itself with more persistency and skill to use the machinery of politics and party. How shall the threatened interests now defend themselves? They can seek to recover some of the positions, constitutional and economic, they had lost. Here is the first meaning of Tariff Reform and of the new legislative claim of the Lords. But Tariff Reform has two purposes. No government in modern times can prevent a constant growth of public expenditure, and modern Conservatism, whether instructive or enlightened, accepts a large and expensive policy of doles to distressed interests, and such 'social reforms' as eleemosynary and police considerations dictate. More money must be found. By indirect taxation the body of the people can best be made to pay their share, and an indirect taxation, which at the same time serves those business interests that are bulwarks of Conservatism, will of necessity be preferred.

It is only when we thus conceive the situation as one which is fundamentally an attack upon and a defence of the present distribution of rights of property, that we can resolve some of the paradoxes that appear upon the surface. Why for instance should the great consuming South uphold Protection, the first effect of which is to raise the prices of consumables, against the producing North? Why, again, should the 'educated' classes hold so lightly the teaching of history that they should be prepared to fling an obsolete constitutional barrier across the flowing stream of popular liberties?

This election presents more plainly than ever before the instinctive rally of the classes and interests, whose possessions, prestige, privileges and superiority of opportunity, are menaced by the new forces of constructive democracy. Landowners are put to the defence of unearned increments and land assessments; licence-owners fear the loss of their monopoly; great manufacturers and employers fear increased taxation of wealth and the legal strengthening of labour organisations; the Church, conscious of the indifference of the working classes to its spiritual authority and fearing disestablishment and disendowment, defends its hold upon the schools; the services are natural allies of force and economic privilege; the Universities fear lest a too utilitarian populace should repudiate their academic values and explode the solemn futilities of a too decorative culture.

In setting this array of Conservative forces against the pressure of the organised workers for economic security and opportunity, as the central fact of present politics, I am no doubt giving a too exclusively materialistic interpretation. The spirit of both parties is also nourished on finer sentiments and less selfish convictions. Everywhere in town and country sturdy Nonconformity has given a moral glow and a crusading enthusiasm to the radical cause, and has infused a religious passion into the demand for the land.

On the other hand the ranks of Conservatism are sustained by a corresponding glow of patriotism, in the feeling that they are defending the very pillars of the social order threatened by disintegrating forces of socialism within and the menace of a foreign enemy without. This genuine sentimentalism half supplements and half conceals the play of the driving and directing forces which animate politics.

One point, in conclusion, deserves particular attention, for it contains the chief justification of democracy. Though I have found a larger play of rationalism and of conscious individual judgment in this election than in any former one, I cannot attribute to this individual rationalism the chief place as determinant. Organisation and intelligent association for common human purposes constitute the strength of civilised society. Where masses of men are thus associated for work and life, there exist the best conditions for the emergence and the operation of that sane collective will and judgment which, in the sphere of politics, constitutes the spirit and the policy of progressive democracy. It is not mere individual self-interest, or more intimate acquaintance with the facts of trade and industry, which leads the Lancashire or Yorkshire mill-operative or the Northumbrian miner to reject the Tariff that seems so alluring to the London clubman or the country vicar or the half-pay officer at Brighton or Bournemouth. There is, I feel sure, a half-instinctive, half-conscious drive of collective wisdom, set up by the associated working class life which the needs of modern capitalistic production have established, a genuine spirit of the people, however incomplete in its expression, which makes for political righteousness.

The intelligence of associated labour is less likely to be led astray by sophistry or sentimentalism than the more cultivated but more individualised intelligence of the scholar, the professional man, or the member of that swell-mob commonly termed 'Society.' Nor is its superiority shown merely in the avoidance of error, an instinct of wholesome Conservatism. From the will of such a people proceeds a constructive political energy, moving somewhat blindly and unevenly, and not with firm persistent direction, towards rather shapeless ideals. It is the creative instinct of the collective mind seeking to express itself in politics, very uncertain in its crude handling of material, groping after ill-conceived effects, wasting much, spoiling some, but learning the art called democracy.

I do not mean to claim that the artisans of the North are 'the people.' In some respects they are very limited in aims and outlook. There may even be a certain danger of a new though wider class government, if their superior organisation enabled them to wield for a while the same measure of dominance in politics as that possessed formerly by the landed aristocracy, or latterly by the mercantile and middle trading classes. I can conceive that collective mechanic mind and will impressing themselves too hardly upon our social institutions, and with too little tenderness towards those above and those below, too rigorous in the regimentation of the weaker grades of workers, shirkers and defectives.. But all the same it is to this associated labour power that we must look for the rudiments of any coming art of democracy, and to my mind the most significant lesson of the election is the geographical and social testimony to the emergence of this popular power.

J. A. HOBSON.

Article 8

CHAPTER VI

FOREIGN INVESTMENTS AND HOME EMPLOYMENT.

AS the saving and investing powers of a nation grow, by reason of improved methods of producing wealth, a larger quantity and a larger proportion of new capital tend to seek investment in foreign countries. Though it must be presumed that the owner of such capital gains by sending it abroad so as to earn for him a higher rate of interest than he could get at home, there are many who maintain that this private gain is attended by a public loss. For, if this capital *Argument against Foreign Investments.* had stayed at home and been applied in some home investment, it would, they urge, have given employment to British labour, and though the wealth it assisted to produce might be slightly smaller than that produced through investing it abroad, there would be caused an increased aggregate of industry and wealth-production in this country.

Investment of capital abroad undoubtedly implies an increase of export trade. For in no other form than that of British goods can British capital go out. An English investor who buys shares in

an Argentina railroad company, or in City of
Osakas, pays for these shares by money which is
nothing else than an order upon British goods.
Defenders of the utility of foreign investments
sometimes make much of the fact that, by float-
The case for
Foreign
Investments.
ing and investing largely in foreign rails or mines,
we secure orders for British engines and
machinery to equip these businesses, and for
British ships to carry out their plant. And this,
no doubt, is true, but it is not really relevant.
From the standpoint of volume of foreign trade
it makes no difference whether the Argentina
railway, whose shares we take up, equips itself
with British or with American engines and rails.
For if Argentina does not take the subscribed
capital in British-made railway plant, it must
take it in other British goods; or, if it does not
do this, it must cause some other foreigners to
buy British goods instead of doing so herself.
Only in one of these ways can a British investment in Argentina be effected. If the cheques
with which British investors buy the Argentina
Effects of
Foreign
Investments on
British Trade.
stocks are converted into orders for British
engines and rails, the nature of the investment
is obvious. But if they are not so converted, it
remains equally certain that the British indebtedness they register can only be met by inducing
some foreigners to buy British goods, whether
rails or cotton goods or ships or other products,
which they would not have bought but for this
British investment in Argentina stocks. How
this compulsion to buy British goods is exerted

through the operations of international exchange I need not here describe. For no business man will dispute the fact that an investment of British money implies an export of British goods, not necessarily at once but ultimately, and usually at no distant date. The capital thus exported will earn a slightly higher rate of interest than it could hope to earn at home, and this interest will be paid in foreign goods which will come in to swell the import trade of this country. Even if the interest is not at once taken in imports, but is left to accumulate by reinvestment abroad, eventually the fruits of this enhanced foreign investment must be taken in foreign goods entering as imports.

Foreign Investments mean Increased Imports.

Now, those who think the free growth of foreign investments injurious to this country find three separate damages accruing from this process.

Charge levelled by Foreign Investment dissenters.

1. It reduces employment and retards industrial development at home.

2. It introduces an increasing quantity of imports which need no exports to pay for them.

3. It equips foreign competitors to compete with us in our own or neutral markets.

It is necessary to set out these charges in more detail before examining their validity.

An article in the "Bankers' Magazine" for November, 1909, upon "Investments, Exports, and Employment" makes the following com-

6

parison between the results of foreign and home
investments :—

"For the time, the effect of investments
abroad has the same influence on the employment of labour in this country as of investments in the United Kingdom. Labour is
set in motion, both to produce the exports
and to transport them to the country to
which the advance is made; the ships in
which the goods are carried have to be built,
manned, and kept in repair. But though this
is the effect at the time, the eventual influence of a foreign investment on the employment of labour is very different, after the
first year or so, from that of an investment
within the four seas. When the investment
is made in this country, it remains either as
a productive instrument continually assisting
our internal trade, in the shape of a railway,
a new tramway, new ironworks, or it may
assist the convenience and prosperity of the
inhabitants in the form of waterworks or
gasworks. These last may not produce a
return in exactly the same way as a new
manufactory does, but they add to the comfort of the inhabitants, as waterworks do,
and they also enable many trades to be
carried on which require a continual water
supply. The same applies to gasworks,
electric works, and many other similar concerns. If only a tenth part of our investment is in domestic undertakings, as appears

Foreign
Investments
and British
labour.

Home
Investments
and British
labour.

to have been the case in 1909, we cannot
wonder at the increase of unemployment and
of distress among the working classes."

Though the income derived from these foreign
investments in the form of dividends may be
somewhat larger than if the money had been
invested at home, the expenditure of this larger
income, it is contended, will afford a very slight
stimulus to British industry and employment as
compared with the application of the capital sum
in home trade.

The reasoning at first sight seems plausible. Trade depres-
Though, as statistics show, the general tendency sion and
migration of
to invest an increasing proportion of our capital Capital.
abroad proceeds irrespective of the state of trade,
it is accentuated in times of depression. But to
charge the migration of capital with being a cause
of home depression and unemployment is to
transpose the true order of causation, putting the
cart before the horse.   An increase of foreign
investment does not cause unemployment and
depression at home; on the contrary, unemployment and depression, involving a reduced demand
for capital at home, drives it abroad.   It is important to establish the truth of the following Capital
Investment:
propositions.   1. In periods of unemployment three
and depression in this country there is no lack Propositions.
of capital for home use.   2. If an attempt were
made to stop capital from going abroad and force
it into home investment, no nett benefit to home
trade would accrue.   3. Foreign investments,
therefore, constitute a useful means of disposal of

a surplus of British capital which remains after the needs of the home investment market are sufficiently met.

The first of these propositions is the crucial one. For if, during a period of trade depression, there is no deficiency of capital, it is idle to argue that it is injurious for capital to go abroad. Now, is it not notoriously the case that, when a period of trade depression sets in, all the important trades of the country are amply supplied with all the capital they want and can profitably use?

So long as capital is treated in an abstract and vague manner as financial power, it may appear that pumping more of this power into a trade will stimulate its vitality. But those who follow this economic interpretation of investment will not be thus deceived. They will recognise that putting capital into a trade means supplying it with more buildings, machinery and other plant, more raw materials, fuel, and other concrete wealth required to co-operate with labour, and such money, or general command of wealth, as is needed to maintain labour until the goods produced by it are marketed. Now, can it be said that any of these forms of real concrete capital is lacking when trade depression sets in? Confronting the unemployed or under-employed labour is unemployed or under-employed plant and machinery, there is usually an abundance of raw materials, and warehouses are glutted with unsaleable goods; all the material apparatus for

Sufficiency of Capital in time of Trade Depression.

Effect of employing Capital for Trade purposes.

making, carrying, and distributing goods exists
not merely in sufficiency but in evident excess.
Is it credit that is lacking?   Though at the
moment of a trade crisis there is a stringency in
the money market with a high price for money,
this is not the case during a depression.   Quite
the contrary; there is an abundance of money in **Trade Depression**
and the Money
the hands of bankers and other financiers, not **Market.**
merely for investment in any home business that
shows promise, but for loans at low rates to manufacturers and traders who can give reasonably
good security, i.e., who can show a probability
that they can use the money to produce goods
which can be profitably sold so as to enable the
borrower to repay the advance he has received.

In the face of these notorious facts, how can it
be contended that there is any lack of productive
capital in a time of trade depression, or that
foreign investments have robbed British industries of the capital required to keep them fully
employed?   The problem of a general depression
of trade, like that of 1908-9, is the problem of a
simultaneous excess of capital and labour, unable
to co-operate for ordinary purposes of production **Causes of**
general Trade
because of an insufficient market for the goods **Depression.**
they could produce.   Every well-informed and
thoughtful business man knows that the crux of
the matter lies in the normal tendency of producing power to outrun the actual rate of consumption, so that periodically the whole productive machinery must be slowed down.   It is no
part of my business here to discuss the causes of

this normal tendency towards over-production, or under-consumption.* For it is sufficient to point out the admitted fact that though in theory it

Excess of Supply over Demand the principal factor in Trade Depression.

should be as easy to sell as to buy, and consumption should always keep pace with production, in practice it works out quite otherwise. Consideration of the actual condition of trade in a depression precludes the serious entertainment of the suggestion that at such times there is any lack of capital in British industries. It is, doubtless, sometimes maintained that even in depressed trade there are some rising new industries insufficiently provided with capital. But those who put forward the hypothesis may be safely challenged to name the trades which at such times, when loanable capital is extraordinarily cheap, are unable to get enough for any reasonably profitable use. Though it is sometimes

Inability of Cheap Money to arrest Trade Depression.

expected that cheap money will suffice to stop a general trade depression by stimulating production and extensions of businesses, there is no evidence that it does in fact so operate to any appreciable extent. Not until the slackening or stoppage of production has gone so far that surplus stocks are gradually cleared and consumption has begun once more to tighten up the reins of industry does a real demand for more capital in home trade become effective.

This being so, it is idle to contend that hampering the process of foreign investment, by differen-

---

* It is discussed at some length in my volume, " The Industrial System " (Longmans).

tial taxation upon their dividends or by any other interference, would be beneficial to British trade and employment, or that it would bring into actual use a larger quantity of home capital.

The desire to obtain the higher rate of interest yielded by foreign investments at such times must be deemed to be a necessary motive for the saving which has brought into existence the capital that seeks this investment. Any artificial impediment would then not simply divert this capital from foreign into home investment : it would stop the creation of this capital.   But, it may be urged, this will only apply in part to capital that goes abroad. Much of this capital, it will be contended, would be willing to take a slightly lower interest at home, if it were not permitted or encouraged to go abroad.   Now, what does this mean in terms of industry?   It means that at a time when there are more cotton factories and iron foundries than are able to get orders it is proposed to build more factories and more foundries and equip them with plant ; that when railway returns are low and traffic falling, more engines and rolling stock shall be provided and necessarily unremunerative branch lines be laid down ; that when overbuilding has everywhere been going on, more buildings shall be put up, and so forth. Now, as we have already seen, this could not to any considerable extent take place. For bankers and other financiers controlling the course of new investment would not dare to embark upon such precarious enterprises at such

Prohibition of Foreign Investments through taxation.

Excess of Capital for Home Investments.

times, would not dare to put up new mills on the chance of their cutting out existing mills in the competition for orders and contracts already insufficient to furnish adequate employment to the capital and labour in the trade. But suppose

Reckless employment of Capital in Home Industries.

that, actuated by some reckless faith in the future they did invest their clients' money in new plant and other business undertakings at such a time, what would be the result? The immediate effect, I agree, would be a stimulus to trade : there would be more employment in the mining, machine-making, railway, building, and other trades engaged in setting up the new factories and other plant. But, seeing that the next effect would be an enhancement of the manufacturing and other productive power, which was already seen to be greater than could find regular, full, and profitable employment, it seems evident that any such addition to this productive power would intensify the malady, and that the temporary stimulus, given so long as the new plant was being set up, would involve an enlargement of the depression as soon as an attempt was made to operate the

Home Industries: effect of over-production.

new manufacturing power. For if the productive power already existing was found to be so much in excess of what was wanted to supply the markets, an increase of this power would glut the markets earlier and more completely. So an artificial stopping of home industries would cause more violent disturbance of the industrial system, involving bigger and more injurious stoppages,

and adding nothing to the aggregate of trade and
employment over a term of years.

Put more simply, this argument means that
foreign investments do not injuriously compete
with home investments, robbing the latter of
capital which it could put to advantageous use in
employing British labour, but that they represent
a use found abroad for a surplus quantity of
British saving, which otherwise would either not
exist at all or would represent a wasteful over-
supply of home capital. It is no reply to say
that there are new electrical, motor car, and other
home industries ready to absorb any amount of
new British capital in developing new industries
for the stimulation and supply of new wants.
These new trades can already get as much capital
as they deserve or can absorb: interference with
foreign investments would not enable them safely
or advantageously to increase their pace of growth.

Foreign Investments represent surplus British savings.

Foreign investments, then, form in the first
instance a safety-valve against excessive gluts of
capital at home. They find a profitable use for
capital which otherwise could not economically
fructify at all. The profits of this use come to
this country in the form of exports. This brings
us to the second grievance of the critics of foreign
investments. They find in the goods which come
into this country in payment of interest on foreign
investment an additional injury to home employment. For, whereas other imports are the means
by which foreigners pay for British goods which
go out to them in export trade, these imports

Profits derived from Foreign Investments.

draw forth no such exports, and so stimulate no corresponding activity in British industries. The receipt of some £120,000,000 worth or more of

Objections of the anti-foreign Investor. such free goods into our markets, however desirable from the standpoint of the consumer, inflicts, they hold, upon the producer two injuries. In the first place, there is the negative injury that he has to send out no goods to pay for them; in the second place, they displace to some extent goods which would have been produced at home by British capital and labour—a positive blow to British industry. The investment of British capital abroad is thus represented as responsible to a larger extent than any other cause for the "dumping" on our shores of large quantities of goods which could and would otherwise have been made at home, employing our capital and labour in their making.

Nor is this the worst. The exportation of capital not merely brings this influx of unpaid-for

Further objection: trade competition. imports, but, by improving foreign countries and equipping them with our best machinery and plant, it makes them formidable rivals of our own producers. Even if it be admitted that the development of the agricultural resources of such lands as Argentina and North-West Canada is justified, in bringing us the abundant supplies of grain needed by a population which, like ours, must supplement its native resources from foreign lands, it cannot be equally serviceable to build up competitors for our manufactures or our carrying trade. With capital that we ourselves supply,

countries such as the United States, Japan, and
India, not to mention countries nearer home, are
enabled, first, to produce for themselves manufactured goods which we used to sell and still
would like to sell them ; secondly, to compete with
us and often to displace our wares in neutral
markets; last, and worst, to invade our own Final counts in
the Indictment.
markets and to undersell our manufacturers.
Such are the further counts of the indictment
against foreign investments as enemies of home
trade and employment.

Before answering them I may remind readers
of the curious dilemma with which they seem to
be confronted. We have already proved that the
capital that goes abroad is not wanted and cannot,
in fact, be utilised at home. It now appears that
it is even more injurious to our trade if it be
allowed to go abroad. Only two other courses
seem open, either not to bring it into existence
or to sink it into the sea. But before adopting
such counsels of despair we will examine more
closely the damages which these investments are
said to inflict upon our trade.

These large quantities of imports, due directly
and indirectly to foreign investments, are Foreign
Investments
benefit the
British
Consumer
obviously advantageous to our consuming public,
whose real incomes are thus raised by the lower
range of prices caused by these accessions to our
home supplies. Since the final object of all
industry is to put consumable goods in the possession of consumers, it may be claimed that this

admission is in itself a sufficient defence of the beneficial nature of foreign investment.

But we may be reminded that we are here arguing the issue from the standpoint of the volume of trade and of employment, and that in such an argument the consumers' interests have no relevancy. Let us then return to the immediate question, viz., whether the foreign investments cause a reduction in the volume of home trade and employment, first, by displacing home-made products in our markets; secondly, by displacing our products in foreign markets.

Now, in the first place it must be remarked that if foreign investments exercised this depressing influence upon home trade, we should expect this depression to be permanent and of increasing intensity, to correspond with the growth, both absolute and relative, of this employment of our capital. For the quantity of imports entering this country as interest upon our foreign capital continually grows, and so does the competing power of foreign nations due to the stimulation of the capital which we provide them. Yet for considerable periods our capital and labour in home industries do not seem to suffer from this invasion, but are able to put forth their full activity in profitable industry. Nor is there any evidence that trade depressions and unemployment are increasing in frequency or intensity in this country, as might be anticipated if this artificially stimulated foreign competition were their cause.

Foreign Investments in relation to Home Trade and Employment.

Trade depression not caused by Investment of Capital abroad.

But this consideration does not in itself dispose of the case against foreign investments. For it might be that this depressing tendency was only realised when a financial crisis, bad harvests, or some other cause, was weakening our markets. It is necessary by direct analysis to face the question whether foreign investments can and do damage our powers to produce and to market our products. Now, here it is material to point out that a very small proportion of our imported goods, whether coming as interest on capital or in ordinary course of exchange, consists of fully manufactured or completed goods, ready to pass into consumption without any use of British industry.   More than three-quarters consist of foodstuffs, materials, and partly manufactured goods.   These, entering as raw materials into many of our staple trades, by their abundance and their cheapness keep down the costs of production of the final products, and by lowering the prices enable us to effect larger sales at home and to secure large foreign markets which we could not have done but for the assistance of these imports.   Even of the 23 per cent of imports classed as mainly or wholly manufactured goods a large proportion figures as "costs" in some home business.   Foreign door-frames or window-sashes cheapen the cost of building and so cause more or larger houses to be built, thus compensating for the loss of home employment which appears to be inflicted on our carpenters.   Even such articles as rolled desks and bicycles are not

Bearing of Foreign Investments upon Home Production.

How imports benefit Home Production.

mere consumers' goods: they figure as "costs" in large numbers of productive and distributive trades: to keep them out would mean some lowering of profits or raising of prices for British made products.

Nor can we ignore the important effect of free importation upon real wages. By helping to keep down the price of foods and of all other consumers' goods, manufactured or other, imports tend to keep down money wages, and so to maintain a lower range of selling prices than would otherwise be possible. This economy is applicable to all British trades, but its most important effect consists in enabling us to secure large and profitable foreign markets, underselling nations which by tariffs, or by lack of imports entering as interest on foreign capital, are subject to higher costs of production.

Economy of free importation.

This defence of the economy of free importation shows that the goods which enter as interest on foreign investments cannot be regarded merely as displacing goods which would otherwise have been made by British industries. Their main effect appears to be stimulative rather than depressive, enabling our industries to turn out larger quantities of goods at lower costs and prices for our own markets and for export trade.

Foreign Investments benefit Home Industries.

This primary economic effect of foreign investments is supported and enhanced by a no less important secondary effect. The main economic object and result of our exportation of capital is to exploit the natural and human resources of

relatively backward countries. By making roads
for them, developing their mines, fields, and
forests, and in due time supplying them with
machinery and other plant for a manufacturing   Economic
                                                 objects of
career, helping to build and equip their cities, and Capital invested
                                                 abroad.
to train and organise an industrial population, we
are undoubtedly raising them towards the same
industrial level as ourselves.   Are we, thereby,
setting up dangerous rivals who will rob us of our
trade, in their market, our market, and neutral
markets?   The hypothesis which underlies this
notion is that there exists at any time only a
limited amount of market, and that increased sales
effected by one competitor imply a corresponding
decline in the sales of another.   Now this conception of trade is fundamentally false.   The first
principle of trade, national or international, is
that of co-operation, or mutual service, not of
rivalry or antagonism. The process of competition
is subordinate to co-operation.   Absorption in   Co-operation the
                                                 first principle
the concrete details of a single trade tends to hide of Trade.
this truth, and has enabled certain persons to
represent the relations between trading nations
as essentially hostile.   The fallacy here is double-
rooted.   There is first the false assumption that
nations as such are economic units, and trade with
one another and with other nations.   Great
Britain, Germany, and the United States are not
trading firms ; they do not bid against one another
for custom ; there are no commercial relations,
except of a subsidiary and indirect kind, between
them.   Certain English firms compete with

certain German and American firms in the markets of these or other countries. So far, however, as such competition involves rivalry and antagonism, it is much keener and more persistent between the several English or the several German firms than between the members of different nations.

The second form of the fallacy is the supposition that it is an advantage for a business man to be surrounded by other business men less prosperous, intelligent, and enterprising than himself. At first sight it may look as if he were the gainer by being so much better off. But this is not really the case. An enterprising and productive man needs neighbours who are enterprising and productive, and that for two reasons. There are many things he wants to buy, and many that he wants to sell. He can buy to the best advantage if his neighbours engaged in various industries are as keen, as enterprising, and as productive as himself. Similarly, he can sell to best advantage if the growing needs and desires of his neighbours are fortified by purchasing power. Every business man knows that it is better to be a member of a prosperous industrial community than of a poor and backward one. What applies to a small applies likewise to a large community. The merely political barriers of States have no power to annul or to restrict this economy, the advantage of having large numbers of rich and prosperous neighbours. No doubt every individual trader would like to be the only

Advantage of equality of business ability.

Mutual prosperity essential in business.

prosperous trader in his particular line, and to
have large numbers of prosperous neighbours in
other lines. But this condition he cannot realise,
and if he could it would not really be to his advantage, for it would remove that healthy stimulus
of competition essential to industrial progress.

If, then, it be admitted that an English firm
gains by having plenty of other prosperous firms
all about the country, even though some of these Competition
firms are in its own line, similarly it gains by and co-operation
having prosperous firms in other countries from in business.
which to buy and to which to sell. In other
words, the detailed antagonism of competitors in
one's own trade is a consideration subsidiary to
the gain of having the effective co-operation of
prosperous businesses in other trades.

This is only another way of saying that trade
is a mutual exchange of goods and services, and
that it is better to have a large number of rich
persons with whom to carry on exchange than
a small number of poor ones.

Once expel the fallacy that nations are trading
units, the application of the doctrine to foreign
investments becomes obvious. For foreign in- Foreign
vestments are a means of enlarging the circle of Investments
business men capable of supplying what we want increase Trade
to buy and of demanding what we want to sell. operations.
The fact that some of these business men get
business away from us is a comparatively small
and incidental drawback to this great economy
arising from an effective expansion of the area
of prosperous exchange.

7

The interest which comes back to this country from foreign investments is not the only great gain which comes to the members of our nation from this process. The opening up and develop-

Development of Foreign and Colonial Trade by exportation of Capital. ment of North and South America, of India, Australasia, and of other countries which have sucked up our surplus capital, has meant an enormous increase in the incomes derived from our home industries and in the purchasing power of these incomes. In the development of these countries by our capital we are building up new customers for our goods and new sources of supply for what we need to buy. As they thus develop, they will display powers to supply to themselves, to us, and to the world, certain sorts of goods better or more cheaply than we can, so driving our home industries gradually out of these branches of production into others that yield products which enable us to buy from them upon terms more advantageous to us, the goods we formerly produced. The notion that there is a limited number of trades, each of a limited size, and that, therefore, if by developing another country we lose some trades or diminish the size of them, we are damaged in the aggregate of our national

Interdependency of Nations in World-trade. industry, is a fallacy based upon an ignorance of the very nature of trade as an exchange of goods for goods. Under modern conditions of the interdependency of nations in world-trade, it is impossible for any nation to use its improved development and richness of resources so as to injure the aggregate industry and employment of

any other country in commercial relations,
directly or indirectly, with it. Least of all is it
capable of injuring the industries of that country
whose capital has helped to develop its resources
and with which it is compelled by economic
necessity to maintain close relations of exchange.
On the contrary, a country, thus developing, Mutual
cannot keep its gains entirely to itself, but is advantages of Capital invested
forced by sheer self-interest to communicate large in foreign Countries.
parts of them to those who buy from it and sell
to it. Canada and Argentina might like to keep
for their own farmers the full benefits of the rich
virgin wheat lands opened up by British capital.
But they are compelled to give us a considerable
portion of the benefit by cheapening the price of
wheat. And so it is with every sort of wealth
produced in these new countries: the competing
farmers, transport companies, and dealers in these
countries, by the very process of seeking markets
for their goods, are obliged to hand over a large
share of the gains of the development, not merely
to the foreign capitalists in interest, but to all How the
those groups of foreign producers and consumers, distribution of profit is effected.
who have dealings with them. It is not even
necessary that our people should have direct dealings with a foreign country to which we have lent
capital, in order to profit by the development due
to our investment. We might, for instance, in
the not distant future find some parts of China
a very favourable field for investment. But
China might not by this development be able to
sell us any large quantity of goods we wanted, or

to take from us any large quantity of what we have to sell. Even the interest upon the capital they might pay us, not in Chinese wares, but by orders on the goods of Japan, America, or some other country with which they did large trade.

Home Industries and Foreign Development.

But the development of China thus procured might none the less be immensely advantageous to British industries, by furnishing cheap foods or materials to foreign producers in the United States or some other country which was thereby enabled and obliged to sell to us materials or goods which we want for our use on terms advantageous to our industries.

Our relations with South Africa illustrate this important truth, upon one side. Though South Africa is a not inconsiderable purchaser of our manufactures, she has comparatively little to give us that we want. The gold and diamonds which are her chief products for export to indeed pass through our hands, but we do not keep or want to keep the bulk of them for our own use. We retain comparatively little of the fruits of the

How South African development affects Home Industries.

mining and other work our capital has done. The bulk of the interest due to us, of the payment for the British manufactures they buy, and of our share in the general wealth of the country, comes home to us in the shape of foods, materials, and manufactured goods from other countries which among them take the larger share of the gold, diamonds, and other products with which South Africa enters the world market.

The development of a backward country by

foreign capital is always beneficial to the country
itself, to the industrial world at large, and to the
investing country in particular. It is of course
quite conceivable that the greatest gainer, next to
the developed country, might be not the investing
country but some other in closer trade relations
with the former. But for the barriers mutually
established between Canada and the United
States, the industries and people of the latter **Benefit to the
Investing
Country.**
country would probably have reaped a larger
benefit than the people of this country by the
large influx of British capital into the Dominion.
In the long run, indeed, they must be the greater
gainers, though doubtless a large share of the gain
may be attributed to work done or assisted by
their own exported capital.

But, normally, the people and industries of the
investing country stand to gain more than any
other foreign country. For in the first place, a
large part of the concrete capital which goes out
by the process of investment usually consists of
engines, rails, machines, stores, and other equipment, ordered directly from firms in the investing
country. Part, at any rate, of the management of
the railway, mine, irrigation works, or other busi- **Investing
Country the
chief gainer by
exportation of
Capital.**
nesses to which the capital is devoted, is likely
to be in the hands of persons belonging to, or
friendly to, the investing country. Thus the
work of repair, improvement, and extension in the
future, will evoke fresh orders for the investing
country. Moreover, the business and social intercourse involved in these proceedings will be likely

to extend to others: business breeds business and every order smoothes the path for another order. Great Britain in particular has profited by this

Great Britain's supply of concrete Capital.
natural process: her generally sound and reliable goods, especially in the engineering and machine-making trades that figure so largely in the supply of concrete capital, have all over the world helped to pave a broad commercial road for other British manufactures.

The indictment of foreign investment as an injury to home industry and employment thus completely breaks down on examination. The gains to the investing nation are four; first the export trade involved in the process of invest-ment; secondly, the stimuli and food to home industries from the payment of interest, most of

Four gains to the Investing Country.
which comes in foods and materials that lower the " costs " of production in home industry, thus enlarging the home market, and the general export trade; thirdly, the share of the new wealth proceeding to her from the debtor country, directly and indirectly, by the ordinary processes of exchange; fourthly, the special trade relations set up and maintained by the very nature of the financial assistance rendered.

The aggregate of these gains forms an immense positive advantage to home industries and home employment arising out of foreign investments.

CHAPTER VII

POLITICAL AND SOCIAL INFLUENCES OF CAPITAL.

A S the area of investment widens for any class
or nation of investors, their interests and
sympathies expand, and the influence they exert
through public opinion or politics upon the conduct of affairs in the places where they have invested capital becomes a factor of growing importance. Regarded merely as an educational influence, this expansion of the area of investment is
of considerable efficacy. A man whose business
interests are confined within his parish is
parochial in his sympathies and outlook. If, on
the other hand, his trade brings him into touch
with business men in many other towns in his
native country, his country means more to him—
he is a better citizen. Still more is this the case
where trading interest is supplemented by investment and a business man has a "stake" in
a number of industries in various places. Though
his patriotism may be too much a matter of
pocket and his politics too exclusively capitalistic,
it remains true that they will be broader, and

Local influence
exerted by
Investors of
Capital.

more intelligent, and on the whole more conformable to public welfare than the feelings and the policy of the mere parochialist. When trade and investments carry men still further afield, inducing a knowledge and an interest in the affairs of foreign countries, the widening of outlook and of sympathy involved lays the basis of the cosmopolitan, the true "man of the world." This expansion of interest and policy is essential to the success of the modern art of investment, and its

Essentials to Success in modern Art of Investment

political and social implications are of the first importance in the history of modern civilisation.

For the members of one nation who have invested capital in a foreign country possess an interest in everything that may happen in that country to affect the security and the fructification of their capital. So far as any capital they may have invested in their own country is concerned, they can, as individual citizens or by combination, exert an appreciable and definite influence in protecting and improving it, where governmental

Influence of the Home Investor on the Productivity of Capital.

means can be utilised. Though business men who cleave too closely to the principle "Our trade, our politics," may be dangerous citizens, working for a trade, or a class interest in opposition to the welfare of the nation's, their intelligence and influence will serve upon the whole to safeguard and advance the productivity of capital. Apart from the special trade interests which the pull upon a tariff or some particular policy of public expenditure may involve, they will be supporters of good order, education, and improved efficiency of labour, and public development of the natural resources of the country.   This would be the normal attitude of the enlightened capitalist with investments of various kinds in different parts of his own country.

Now the cosmopolitan investor will have the same interest in the good order and development of the countries where his capital lies.   But not being a citizen of those various states he will not be able to exert the same sort of direct influence. Thus, as the numbers of these cosmopolitan capitalists grow and their stakes in countries not their own are larger and more various, the urgency of building up some international political machinery for protecting and promoting their scattered interests becomes continually more evident.   So far as foreign investments depend for their safety and success upon local conditions affected by government there will be a constant growing tendency for investors to seek to influence that foreign government, either privately or by the diplomacy or force of their own government. Examples of such private intervention are the numerous cases where foreign syndicates obtain concessions for railroads, mining or other enterprises by personal negotiation with the government of a country without the assistance of their own government.   The history of the Transvaal and Rhodesia, of China, Egypt, Persia is full of modern instances of private capitalistic negotiations with foreign governments.

But in recent times investors more frequently

Necessity of adequate Protection for Capital invested abroad.

Methods of obtaining Concessions from Foreign Governments.

utilise the diplomacy of their government to assist
them in their negotiations for such concessions,
and the course of foreign politics, especially in
the Far East and in South America, turns more
and more upon this competition of the pressure
of foreign governments on behalf of groups of
investors.   Where investments have been thus
effected, whether with or without governmental

Political influence of Investors in Foreign Countries. aid, the foreign stake in a country is always liable
to involve the intervention of a foreign govern-
ment if the security of the invested capital is
threatened by alleged misgovernment.   Sometimes, indeed, the pressure of investors has taken
shape in private force for the substitution of a
government more amenable to their management.
This has usually happened where foreign investments have been accompanied by a considerable
migration of foreign residents directly interested
in the capital.   The classical instance of such an
operation in recent times is the Jameson raid.

The Transvaal and financial pressure. But the whole history of the Transvaal during
the decade preceding the South African war is
illustrative of the pressure brought to bear upon
a foreign government by private groups of financiers for the protection and improvement of their
investments, mostly by personal negotiations with
ministers, but partly by diplomatic pressure of
the European governments.

As foreign trade and foreign investment
advance it becomes a more important and more
useful function of every government to try to
secure for its citizens new markets for their goods

and for their capital, and to employ public
diplomacy and force to improve the markets
already got and the capital already invested. As
a number of civilised nations enter more largely
and on more equal conditions into foreign trade
and foreign investments, the foreign policy of
their governments is more directly and consciously
engaged in looking after these commercial and
financial interests.   Not merely are definitely
commercial treaties formed to further these interests, but the political relations between nations
are influenced, often predominantly, by considerations of finance. Russia's political alliances, to
name a notorious case, have been dictated in the
frankest manner by the necessity of public loans.

Political relations of Governments influenced by financial considerations.

But, where the borrowing country does not
rank on a political level with the creditor country,
the more usual case, the investment bond commonly leads not to an alliance but to some closer
political control.   Where the citizens of a powerful advanced state have invested largely in a
weaker backward state, either in its public funds
or by way of private enterprise, there constantly
arise opportunities for the investors to press their
government to interfere with the government of
the backward state on their behalf.   The properties which represent these investments may be
actually in jeopardy, the foreign government may
refuse adequate protection or may even confiscate
the capital.   In such cases it is recognised that
the government whose citizens are thus plundered
will intervene, if it has the power to do so.

Government intervention on behalf of Foreign Investors.

Where no such actual peril exists, there is a natural tendency by misrepresentations to secure the intervention of a strong government, if it is believed that the financial value of the shares will be thereby enhanced.

The growing practice of the government of strong advanced capitalistic nations to engage upon the modern process of imperial expansion is chiefly explained by the pressure of the investing classes for larger and safer areas of profitable investment. Other motives co-operate, the impulse towards emigration and the natural desire to keep emigrants under the flag, the desire for secure and preferential markets for the export trade, for mere territorial aggrandisement, or the mission of civilisation. But the main driving force which leads strong modern states to assert political influence and control over weaker states is the bond of financial investment. As the pressure of surplus capital beyond the national confines becomes greater and proceeds from a number of national sources, the use of its government by each national group of investors becomes more exigent and the competition for the best investments more keen. So we see all over the world, but particularly in Asia, foreign policy turning more and more upon the acquisition of spheres of preferential exploitation for railroads, banks, and other development work. By diplomacy, menace, and, in the last resort, by force, each government strives to obtain a " proper share " of each new field of exploitation for its own in

Desire for Imperial Expansion the outcome of Investment.

The bond of Financial Investment.

vestors. Egypt, Asia Minor, Persia, China, S. America, are primarily fields of investment, and the foreign politics which have relations to such countries are primarily determined by the financial considerations which lurk in the background of every national policy. Though other factors, dynastic, racial, religious, humanitarian, overlay and often conceal the play of financial motives, no candid student of the forces which have brought the countries named above into the sphere of interest or control of Western Powers can hesitate to trace the determinant acts mainly to financial causes.

Financial considerations the principal factor in Foreign policy.

At first sight this appears to imply that foreign investments are of necessity a disruptive influence, making for war. On the one hand, they incite strong advanced nations to bring within their political control, as spheres of interest, protectorates, or possessions, those weak and backward territories where their investors have acquired a heavy capitalistic stake, using whatever force is necessary to compass this imperialistic end. On the other hand, they appear to engender enmity and strife between the Powers which eye with jealousy the financial preserves seized by one of their number, and are driven to bitter diplomatic quarrels over each new promising area of investment that shows on the financial horizon, Morocco, Persia, Manchuria, China. "Modern wars are almost all for markets" it has been said, and if we lump together commercial

The possibility of National conflict through Foreign Investments.

and financial interests, it is not far from the truth.

This bellicose interpretation of investments seems also to be supported by the large part played by governmental loans employed to finance armaments and actual wars. No backward state, however large in territory and in population, could engage in a first-class modern war, or make the necessary preparation for it, without the use of international credit. The urgent need of such credit has been, as we have seen, a chief guiding influence in the foreign policy of Russia. The machinery of national and international investment appears to feed the war-spirit among nations by enabling them to furnish themselves with more gigantic and costly instruments of war than they could provide out of the current public revenue, and to wage wars upon a scale only rendered possible by the elaborate mechanism of modern credit.

Government loans for war purposes.

Thus it would appear that investment, like commerce itself, instead of being a bond of peace, may be a source of strife between nations. Cobden too confidently held that growing commercial intercourse between the members of different nations must soon make war impossible, because the injury to both nations attendant on a breach of peace would be so obvious. The " fight for markets " did not enter his mind as a possibility. So it might seem that the naturally pacific tendencies of international finance can be perverted into incendiary forces. Indeed, international finan-

Cobden's mistaken view regarding international commerce.

ciers are sometimes represented as ghouls egging
on weak but ambitious governments with tempt-
ing loans to furnish themselves with warships and
to embark upon perilous careers of aggression.

There is without doubt a large element of truth
in these representations of the aggressive and
provocative influences of international investment. Though war is nearly always injurious to
the economic welfare of both nations that engage
in it, there may be groups of capitalists within
these nations, or in other nations, who stand to
gain by the expenditure which wars involve.
Though the South African war cost our nation
enormous sums, a few groups of mining shareholders calculated they would gain by it, and a
very few perhaps did gain.

Economic welfare of nations retarded by Political Disturbances.

Indeed, it is not right to shirk the peril involved
in the unstable and irrational relations which subsist between public and private finance. So long
as private investors who have put their capital in
an ill-governed and insecure country at rates of
interest which discount the insecurity are enabled
to induce their own government to spend the
public money in order to force a better government upon the country where their investments
lie, the pressure of bondholders will continue to
be a source of war. So long as valuable new areas
of investment are practically kept by governments
as special preserves for companies of investors
exclusively belonging to the nation with political
control, such finance will be provocative of strife
between nations.

Causes of national contention.

These are the defects and dangers attending the development of modern finance up to the present stage. But the new and growing tendencies of a genuinely international finance must continually tend to diminish them and to substitute pacific motives. Though Cobden was too optimistic in attributing to the growth of foreign trade so early and so complete an efficacy as peacemaker, he was correct in his judgment of the tendency. A large and regular trade between members of two nations does modify the temper of their governments; a nation hesitates to seek to injure a good customer or to deprive itself of a good market for the articles its members need for home consumption and home industries. This genuinely pacific influence offsets, perhaps exceeds, the friction which may arise where the traders of two countries seek through their governments to secure a monopoly or preference of some neutral market. But the cross ownership of capital involved in international investment is a far stronger and steadier pledge of peace. When a group of investors, all members of a single nation, England or Germany, or the United States, puts a large amount of capital into developing a backward or an insecure country, this sort of foreign investment may induce an act of aggression or imperial expansion with the object of improving the investment, by obtaining political control over the country in question. But, even here the tendency will always be to

Flourishing trade the desire of every nation.

Cross ownership of foreign invested Capital.

gain their end by diplomatic or other pressure short of war.

Where the international character of an investment has been further marked by the substantial participation of investors of several nationalities, there will not be either the same temptation or the same ability to induce a government to bring pressure upon a foreign state in the interest of financiers, many of whom are not its own subjects. It is true that occasionally co-operation of several Powers, acting in the interests of international finance, has been attempted in China, Venezuela, and elsewhere. But the absence of a close identity of interests, indeed the probability of conflicts of interest between the co-operating Powers, makes for pacific settlement. It is evidently not the interest of a creditor country to inflict upon a debtor country the enormous material injuries involved in modern war. While, therefore, some grave insult or some policy of confiscation practised by a debtor country may still bring a forcible intervention of the creditor country, the international distribution of financial interests renders even this less feasible.

Government pressure in the interest of Financiers.

An illustration of this is furnished by the easy way in which the United States, by a firm parade of its Monroe doctrine, was enabled a few years ago to stop the several European governments whose subjects had interests in Venezuela, from applying force to collect their debts.

The Monroe doctrine in operation.

The Monroe doctrine itself, indeed, has been transformed in a most interesting manner from a

8

political into a primarily financial policy. So far
as South America is concerned, it signifies that
the United States furnishes a partial guarantee
for the security of foreign capital invested in the
southern republics, by undertaking the exclusive
duty of keeping public order and inducing would-
be recalcitrant creditors to "pay up." Though
this obligation has political implications as well,
it is primarily economic, tending to mark out large
tracts of South America as special fields for
American investment. But this financial protectorate, thus asserted by a first-rate power, will
certainly assist the general development of South
American resources through international finance,
and by securing these states against such fili-
bustering expeditions as that of Napoleon III. in
Mexico, or against the political ambitions which
Germany might otherwise have been led to entertain, it will tend to keep the peace over a large
and a turbulent section of the world in which
European investors are very largely interested.

Monroe doctrine and the security of Foreign Capital.

Recent developments in the Far East are
making against the marking out of separate
spheres of trading and exploiting influence in
China and Manchuria for the traders and investors
of the several European nations, which was the
accepted policy of the nineties. For though the
government of each interested power—Russia,
England, Germany, France, and the United States
—still manœuvres for railway and mining concessions for its own syndicates, there is no longer
any hope of the break-up and parcelling-out

Trading spheres of the Far East.

schemes of the period before Japan became a
recognised power. The new diplomacy for the
development of Manchuria shows constant new
shifts and combinations of political and financial
bodies. The recent business arrangement
between Russia and Japan for carrying forward a
comprehensive railway system, if successful, Effect of the Russo-Japanese
would furnish a constantly solidifying basis of railway scheme
peace between the two hitherto opposed aggres- or. Foreign Capital.
sive powers, while the finance for such a project
would of necessity engage the co-operation of
other European nations. For neither Russia nor
Japan can find the requisite capital out of its own
resources. The opposing policy, in which the
United States has taken the lead, aiming at the
construction of railways by an international syndicate, though defeated for the moment, probably
represents the line to which events point in the
future, not merely for Manchuria, but for the
larger Chinese problem, which ranks as the
greatest capitalistic proposition of the near future.

The political break-up of China is no longer
indicated as a probable event. On the other
hand, the rapid strides made in education and in
the study of western sciences and arts is a sure Important economic
precursor to great economic changes, involving an advance in China
organised endeavour to discover, develop, and use foreshadowed.
the vast mineral resources which certain Chinese
provinces possess, and to construct the modern
roads and manufactories which shall bring this
vast population into the ring of civilised industrial
nations. Though it is tolerably certain that in

this work the business of administration will be in the hands of the Chinese, the Oriental people best adapted to a business life, the initial operations of finance for some time to come must involve a large flow of capital from Europe and America. While the United States, in her new capacity of foreign trader and investor, turning ever more consciously to the Pacific for markets and investments, will probably apply a forceful diplomacy to secure Asiatic business for the financial groups who govern the great republic, neither they nor other western peoples will be able to pursue a selfish national policy very far. For when world-confidence in China as a field of investment is once fairly established, the suckage of capital will involve international finance upon a larger scale than has ever yet been practised. This large joint interest will afford the surest basis of peace, at any rate for a generation, in the Far East. Though other motives, non-economic, may eventually bring about an organised endeavour to expel western control, financial as well as political, from the Far East, and to revert to a separatist civilisation, a prolonged utilisation of western capital will afford the strongest guarantees of a period of pacific development, in which all the creditor nations of the world will take their share of profitable exploitation.

China the future area for Capital Investment.

International finance in the Far East a guarantee of Peace.

Imperialism, therefore, regarded as political domination of lower or backward peoples, primarily impelled and directed by desire for profitable trade, or in more recent times for profit-

able areas of national investment, is changing its
character, especially in relation to South America
and the Far East, the two most important fields Imperialism and Foreign Investments.
of financial exploitation. The distinctively
political and nationalist aspect is weakening and
giving way to an economic internationalism exercised with very little direct assumption of political
control, the minimum in fact that is found necessary to afford good security for the international
assets.

The entrance of the United States to a front
place among foreign investors will probably consolidate this tendency. For the early experiments in American imperialism have proved
neither profitable nor popular, and though governmental pressure may be carried far in order to
prevent the closing of foreign areas to American
trade and capital, it is unlikely that the United
States will enter on any further scheme of territorial aggrandisement. A more or less formal
coalition of American republics under the hege- Foreign Investment policy of the United States.
mony of the United States, and a naval policy
in the Pacific, confined to the maintenance of an
open door for American goods and capital, appear
to express the present interests and aspirations of
the ruling forces in the United States. This
milder imperialism is of a definitely pacific character, likely both to promote good order and
development among the backward nations and to
assuage the jealousies of the great powers. Unless
some reckless racial animosity should overpower
the operation of these economic motives, Great

Britain and the United States, directing their efforts primarily to freedom and security of investments in these great areas, will act as the leading channels for a finance which will become continually more cosmopolitan, so far as the ownership of the capital is concerned. Thus, we recognise how, in the relations between advanced and backward nations, the possession and utilisation of capital, placed by members of the former in the countries belonging to the latter, makes more for peace and good government in proportion as the finance grows more distinctively international.

International finance the path to peace and Government efficiency.

Not less striking is the pacific tendency of finance in the relations of the advanced nations themselves. In a very striking book entitled "The Great Illusion," the author dwells upon the revolutionary change effected in the motives and results of war by the advance made in recent times towards a financial solidarity of interests among the capitalist classes of the leading nations. For the successful army of a European country to invade a neighbouring country in order to raid its treasure, destroy its fixed property, and kill its industries, would not merely be a bootless policy, it would be a suicidal one. For the damage it would inflict upon the finance, the industry, and commerce of its own people, would be only second in extent to that inflicted on the enemy.

Peaceful v. warlike methods in Finance.

Suppose a victorious Germany army landed on our shores, proceeded, after ancient usage, to march on London and to loot the cellars of the

Bank of England, the only substantial treasure
in the country,

    " What would be the result of such an
action on the part of a German army in
London? The first effect, of course, would **Effect on British finance of a German invasion of England.**
be that, as the Bank of England is the banker
of all other banks, there would be a run on
every bank in England, and all would suspend
payment.   But simultaneously, German
bankers, many with credit in London, would
feel the effect; merchants the world over,
threatened with ruin by the effect of the
collapse in London, would immediately call
in all their credits in Germany, and German
finance would present a condition of chaos
hardly less terrible than that in England.   It
is as certain as anything can be that, were
the German army guilty of such economic
vandalism, there is no considerable institution
in Germany that would escape grave damage;
a damage in credit and security so serious as **Effect of German invasion on its own finance.**
to constitute a loss immensely greater than
the value of the loot obtained.   It is not
putting the case too strongly to say that for
every pound taken from the Bank of England
German trade would suffer a thousand. The
influence of the whole finance of Germany
would be brought to bear on the German
Government to put an end to a situation
ruinous to German trade, and German
finance would only be saved from utter
collapse by the undertaking on the part of the

German Government, scrupulously to respect private property and especially bank reserves."

Nor would the effect of extorting a heavy war indemnity be fraught with much lighter risks and damages to the victor. Suppose England to have vanquished Germany and to be in a position to extort from her the full costs of such a war:

Financial
result of
raising a War
Indemnity.

" What would be the financial effect throughout the world of draining Germany of, say, five hundred million pounds in gold. In the attempt to secure this gold widespread and ruthless borrowing would have to take place on the part of German financial institutions. The bank rate would go up to such an extent that the recent Wall Street trouble would not be a circumstance to it. But a 7 or 8 per cent bank rate, prolonged throughout Europe, would involve many a British firm in absolute ruin, and a general loss enormously exceeding five hundred million

Financial
influence
against War
Indemnity.

pounds. Such would be the condition of things throughout the world that the leaders of finance in London, which is the financial centre of the universe, would, it is absolutely certain, throw all their influence against, not for, the exaction of a great indemnity from Germany."

Even supposing, that, to avoid the patent folly of such a sudden operation, the payment of the indemnity were spread over some years, the dislocation of world finance and a particular injury to the finance and business of England would ensue, while the heavy taxation which Germany would be obliged to impose upon her people would cripple her power as a large customer of British goods, retard her industrial development, thus reducing her supply of the goods our people wanted to buy from her, and would prevent her from applying her share of capital in opening up South America and other countries whose development is so beneficial to our commerce and our investments.

Increased taxation for War Indemnity purposes.

Every decade the linkage of financial and commercial interests across political frontiers grows so much stronger and more complex that the direct material recoil of war becomes graver and more obvious. Nations in the modern business world cannot, any more than individuals, live to themselves alone. Modern finance is the great sympathetic system in an economic organism in which political divisions are of constantly diminishing importance. Of course, so long as governments, and the public force and money which they handle, can be utilized by private syndicates, either to procure profitable concessions or to improve the marketable value or the yield of properties in foreign lands, the political factor will be liable to be introduced in emergencies. Investors, like traders, will tend to group themselves on such occasions under their flag, striving to cover their profit-seeking deals under some cloak of national policy. But so far as the relations of the civilized powers with one another

Tendency of Modern Finance towards Peace.

are concerned, the growing community of business interests, which the international web of finance involves, is the most solid pledge and the aptest instrument for the preservation of peace.

It will, no doubt, be justly said that our argument assumes for its full efficacy a larger measure of reason and of calculated policy than history discloses in any nation, that nations goaded to fury by some insult or deluded by some reckless statesman, may throw the plainest dictates of self-interest to the wind, risking all the damages which we have enumerated. But as the cost of war increases, there is good evidence that nations are more apt to count it. The appalling ruin which a war between great European powers would bring, not only to the participants, but to the bystanding nations entangled by innumerable bonds of business with one or other of the combatants, is sufficiently well realised by the solid business classes in every nation to yield a very potent public feeling against war. It is this reasonable caution that, far more than any humanity or timidity, has given, through The Hague Conventions and the growing use of arbitration, substance to what, a generation since, were but vague and pious aspirations of philanthropists. That which Christianity, justice, and humane sentiment have been impotent to accomplish through nineteen centuries of amiable effort, the growing consolidation of financial interests, through bourses, loans, companies, and the other machinery of investment, seems likely within a

(margin note) Increasing cost of War an assurance of greater Peace.

(margin note) Consolidation of Financial Interests opposed to Warfare.

generation or two to bring to consummation, namely, the provision of such a measure of effective international government as shall render wars between great civilised powers in the future virtually impossible.

Not merely a handful of great financiers and merchants have important interests in other countries whose safety and prosperity they therefore prize. Thousands of middling citizens, manufacturers, tradesmen, professional men, even clerks and employees, in England, Germany, United States, or France, have interests, as owners of securities, in the welfare of one another's country. A rupture between any two of these countries would come home at once to active business men in every city or town of Great Britain or of Germany as a damage to their outlying properties. For modern international finance means that Germany, as an economic asset, does not belong entirely to the Germans, but that parts of it belong to Britons, while parts of Britain, on the other hand, belong to Germans. Both, moreover, are largely interested in securities in other countries, all of which are liable to suffer damage if Germany and Britain quarrelled with one another, or failed to exert their joint influence to bring other quarrelling nations to a pacific settlement of their disputes. What applies to the case of Germany and Great Britain applies, of course, with varying degrees of intensity to the relations of other powers. In one or two

Cosmopolitan character of Foreign Investors.

Pacific qualities of International Investment.

instances, as that of France and Russia, the direct financial bonds are so tight as to make a rupture incredible.

But everywhere the growth of a network of direct and indirect financial interdependency offers a considerable guarantee for peace. There will doubtless remain subordinate, though not inconsiderable, monetary interests which feed international hostility, financing debts for military and naval equipment, sustaining the shipbuilding, gunmaking, and other industries which live on profitable government contracts for armaments, or seeking speculative profits through the violent oscillations of credit brought about by strains of international relations. But, perilous as is this play of interested or reckless finance, it has less power than is sometimes ascribed to it. For even those interests which thrive on armaments and international unsettlement would generally be losers by actual war, and will help to pull up on the brink of such a precipice. The main current of finance, drawing its sustenance from the security and productiveness of transport, industrial operations and material development of civilised life in the various countries of the world, demands peace and stability of government as first conditions of its free and profitable flow. War, fear of war, and political unsettlement, on the one hand, retard the growth of surplus wealth out of which savings can be made, checking the stimulus to create capital, upon the other, limit the areas of profitable investment, and reduce the efficiency of the work of world-development which international finance exists to carry on.

The hostile element in Finance in the minority.

Investors' need of efficient Government.

Article 9

CHAPTER IX

THE OPEN DOOR

So far I have discussed the New Protectionism as a complicated form of folly. But it is more than that. It is a crime—I had almost written *the* crime — against civilization. For its effect, as its intention, would be to perpetuate the present strife by stamping the divisions made for war upon the world of commerce afterwards. Whereas the whole trend of civilization has been to bind the peoples of the world into closer unity of interests and activities by the growing interdependence of commerce, these proposals are directed to a reversal of the movement. Not merely do they seek to cut across the whole delicate network of commercial and human intercourse, but they make precisely that severance which is most injurious to the future of humanity. To break Europe into two hostile and rival economic bodies, intriguing against one another in all the neutral countries of the world, would be to endow with permanency the political system of contending alliances, which has been the chief cause of past in-security. This political antagonism would be loaded with economic interests which, once established, would be very difficult to displace. The question of the just deserts of Germany and the desire to impose upon her economic punishment are not a real issue. For we have seen that the constitu-tion and working of modern commerce are such as to disable Protection, or other modes of commercial severance, from inflicting any injury which does not equally recoil upon the party inflicting it. Nor are the private sensibilities and animosities of Britons who desire to have no commercial dealings in the future with Germany in question. No trading firm or individual in this country is precluded from putting into operation on his

own behalf a complete boycott of German
goods. It is his desire to impose his policy
upon other firms and other persons, who
may still wish to seek their advantage by
buying and selling in the best market that
is in question.

The adoption of a State policy which, by
stopping all healing intercourse between the
members of the belligerent groups, would
keep alive and exacerbate all the bitterest
memories of war, would be nothing short
of treason against the cause of civilization.
For commerce has always been the greatest
civilizer of mankind. All other fruits of
civilization have travelled along trade routes.
The caravans which crossed the great Asiatic
plains, the boats which conducted the earliest
commerce up and down the great river
courses, carried the first seeds of science,
religion, art, law, and of mutual understanding and good-will, among ever-widening
circles of mankind. Cut off commerce, and
you destroy every mode of higher intercourse. Substitute commercial war for fre-

exchange, and you reverse the current of all civilization and drive back to barbarism.

The full pacific virtues of Free Trade and the constructive policy which it requires have seldom yet been recognized, even by professed Free Traders. This is due to a failure fully to appreciate the profound change that has come about in the economic internationalism of the last half-century. Trade, in its simple meaning of exchange of goods for goods, does not cover the new industrial, commercial, and financial relations between members of different countries. Cobden was admittedly mistaken in thinking that the perception of their obvious self-interest must rapidly lead all other nations in the world to liberate their trade as we had done, and that this universal Free Trade would afford security against future war. His error lay in failing to perceive that, though the interest of each people as a whole lay in freedom of commerce, the interests of special groups of traders or producers within each country would continue

to lie along the lines of privilege and protection, and that until democracy became
a political reality these organized group
interests might continue to mould the fiscal
policy of their several States.

But though this consideration has retarded
the pacific influence of commerce, it has not
been a direct and potent influence for international dissension. While the refusal of
nations to open their markets on equal
terms to foreigners retards and chills friendship, it does not normally promote hostility.
It is the struggle for colonies, protectorates,
and concessions in undeveloped countries,
that has been the most disturbing feature
in modern politics and economics. Foreign
policy in recent decades has more and more
turned upon the acquisition of business advantages in backward parts of the world,
spheres of commerce, influence, and exploitation, leases, concessions, and other privileges,
partly for commerce, but mainly for the
profitable investment of capital. For it is
the export of capital, the wider and more

adventurous overflow of the savings of the capitalists of the developed Western countries, that constitutes the new and dominant factor in the modern situation. Larger and larger quantities of capital are available for overseas investment, and powerful, highly organized firms and groups of financiers seek to plant out these savings in distant lands, where they can be loaned to spendthrift monarchs or ambitious Governments, or applied to build railways, harbours, or other public works, to open and work mines, plant tea, rubber, or sugar, or to serve the general money-lending operations which pass under the name of banking. Many hundreds of millions of pounds during recent years have been flowing from the creditor nations of Europe into this work of "development," which forms the main material ingredient in what is sometimes called the "march," sometimes the "mission," of civilization among backward peoples.

It is the competition between groups of

business men, financiers, and traders, in the
several nations, using the offices of their
respective Governments to assist them in
promoting these profitable business enterprises, that has underlain most of the
friction in modern diplomacy and foreign
policy, and has brought powerful nations
so often into dangerous conflict. To
prove this statement, one has only to name
the countries which have been the recent
danger-areas : Egypt, Morocco, Tripoli,
Transvaal, Persia, Mexico, China, the Balkans. Though in every case other considerations, racial, political, dynastic, or religious,
are also involved, sometimes more potent in
the passions they evoke, the moving and
directing influences have come from traders,
financiers, and bondholders. Through the entanglements of Anglo-French political policy
in Egypt runs the clear, determinant streak
of bondholding interests. The kernel of the
Moroccan trouble was the competition of
the Mannesmann and the Schneider firms
over the " richest iron ores in the world."

Mining financiers moulded the policy of South Africa towards annexation of the gold reef. Tripoli was in essence a gigantic business coup of the Banco di Roma. In Mexico history will find a leading clue to recent disturbances in the contest of two commercial potentates for the control of oil-fields. Persia came into modern politics as an arena of struggle between Russian and British bankers, seeking areas of profitable concessions and spheres of financial influence. In China it was the competition for railroads and for leases and concessions, followed by forced pressures, now competing, now combining to plant profitable loans. Turkey and the Balkans became an incendiary issue to Western Europe because they lay along the route of German economic penetration in Asia, a project fatally antagonized by Russian needs for " free " Southern waters.

The pressure of demand from organized business interests for preferential economic opportunities in backward countries is the driving force behind the grievances and aspirations of thwarted nationalism, political ambition, and imperialistic megalomania. A recent writer* has thus condensed these facts of history : " It is essential to remember that what turns a territory into a diplomatic problem is the combination of natural resources, cheap labour, markets, defencelessness, corrupt and inefficient government."

If the Free Trade policy is to fulfil its mission as a civilizing, pacifying agency, it must adapt itself to the larger needs of this modern situation. Free Trade is indeed the nucleus of the larger constructive economic internationalism ; but it needs a conversion from the negative conception of *laissez faire*, *laissez aller*, to a positive constructive one. The required policy must direct itself to secure economic liberty and equality not for trade alone, but for the capital, the enterprise, and the labour, which are required to do the work of development in all the backward countries of the earth, whether those coun-

* Mr. Lippmann, " The Stakes of Diplomacy," p. 93.

tries "belong to" some civilized State or
are as yet independent countries. This
fuller doctrine of the Open Door, or equality
of economic opportunity, cannot, however,
be applied without definite co-operative
action on the part of nations and their
Governments.

This needs plain recognition. For to some
who have perceived the dangerous diplomatic
emergencies arising from the support given
by Governments to the private business
ventures of their nationals it has appeared
the easiest escape to advocate a doctrine of
mere political disinterestedness. Let Governments give their traders, investors, and financiers, to understand that, while they are at
liberty to enter any business relations they
like with the members or the Governments of
other nations, they are not empowered to
call upon their Government for assistance,
either in establishing or pushing such business, or in redressing any injuries which may
be done to them or their property interests.
Such business, unauthorized by Government

and undertaken for private profit, must carry its own risks. Why, it is asked, should persons who have staked their property in countries where they know the Government to be corrupt, the administration of law to be uncertain, the treatment of foreigners to be unjust, and who presumably have discounted these very risks in the terms of their investments or their trade, be at liberty to call upon their Governments to use the public resources of their country to rescue them from these risks and to improve the value of these private speculations? The logic of this attitude appears irrefutable. But the politics are utterly unpractical and inconsistent with humanitarian progress. No Government has ever maintained, or can ever maintain, a merely disinterested attitude towards the trade or other economic relations of its nationals with foreigners. Governments admittedly are concerned with the industry and commerce, foreign as well as domestic, of their respective peoples, obtaining for that industry and commerce such conditions as may secure for private effort and enterprise the best results. In this capacity they have always been accustomed to use the diplomatic machinery to secure for their "national" trade such liberties and opportunities in foreign lands as are attainable by arrangement with foreign Governments. Most of these arrangements consist in the removal or abatement of legal, fiscal, or other "artificial" restrictions, or in promoting the general safety of life and prosperity of their nationals. This work, done by diplomatic intercourse, special treaty stipulations, consular representations, etc., is work done by the State for the interest of the public as a whole. It is designed to strengthen and improve the commercial and other relations between the countries in question. But since this business is, in fact, conducted by certain firms or persons, whose interests are particularly engaged in it, the benefits of this State action are directly and chiefly reaped by them, and come home in enlarged private gains. But no one can advocate the total abstention of Governments from this work, on the ground that its direct gains are not equally distributed throughout the nation, but are of more advantage to certain individuals and classes than to others. The general effect of this consular and other Governmental action is to secure larger and freer opportunities for trade and investment for all members of the nation capable of engaging in such business, and some of the value of these enlarged business opportunities comes home to the nation as a whole in its capacity of a " consuming public."

It is doubtless a more controversial issue how far it is legitimate for a Government to employ political pressure to assist or advance the particular claims or interests of a firm or syndicate pushing a special financial deal, or contract, or concession, upon the Government or people of a foreign country, or to confer the semi-official authority of a charter upon a company claiming a monopoly of trade or developmental activities in some

10

" backward area." But these practices have been so deep-set in the grooves of history that it is impossible to expect from any State a simple policy of renunciation. Business men have always looked to their Governments to secure for them fair or, if possible, preferential opportunities in business with foreign countries, and they have never looked in vain. Upon the whole, it would be urged, this policy of pushful business, aided by political support, has made for enlarged and freer commercial intercourse, and has been essential in the work of developing distant markets and more remote resources. It is inconceivable that Great Britain or any other civilized nation would be willing to renounce such political aids while other nations still retained them. Is it more conceivable that all Governments by simultaneous agreement should stand aside, giving no more support to their nationals in foreign trade or investments? Yet nothing can be more certain than that this competing support of Governments to foreign business enterprises of their countrymen must, if it continues, ripen new dangerous diplomatic situations, and form the substance of conflicting foreign policies and competing armaments. No League of Nations, no Hague Conventions, or other machinery for settling international disputes, are likely to furnish any reasonable security for peace or for reduced armaments, unless this problem of conflicting interests in the profitable exploitation of new markets and backward countries can be solved. Now there is only one line along which solution is possible. We cannot revert to strictly private enterprise, Governments looking on with folded arms, while private companies, with armed forces of their own, fasten political and economical dominion upon rubber or oil or gold fields in Africa or South America, enslaving or killing off the native population, as in San Thomé or Putumayo, and using up the rich natural resources of the country in a brief era of reckless waste. The only alternative is to advance to a settled policy of international arrangement for securing, if possible, that this commercial and developmental work shall in the future be conducted on a basis of pacific co-operation between the business groups in the respective countries under the joint control of their Governments.

This process of economic penetration and expansion cannot stop.   As more nations advance farther along the road of capitalist industry, the overflows of trade and capital, seeking more distant and more various fields of enterprise, will be stronger in their pressure.   This pressure has been the driving force in the modern Imperialism of the Western nations, stimulating them to discover " spheres of legitimate aspiration," " spheres of influence," " protectorates," " colonies," " places in the sun," and forcing their Governments into dangerous situations.   The process cannot stop.   But it may be possible to extract from it the poisonous sting of international rivalry. Why should not these necessary economic processes of expansion and development be carried on by pacific international arrangements ? The germs of such arrangements are to be found in the Congo Conference of Berlin in 1884-85, in which were represented England, Germany, Austro-Hungary, Belgium, Denmark, Spain, the United States, France, Italy, Holland, Portugal, Russia, Sweden-Norway, Turkey. " This Conference stipulated freedom of commerce, interdiction of slave-trade, and neutralization of the territories in the Congo district, and secured freedom of navigation on the Rivers Congo and Niger."* A somewhat similar international agreement was made, first in 1880 at the Madrid Convention, afterwards in 1906 at the Algeçiras Convention for the economic internationalization of Morocco. Though in the earlier Convention only the nations immediately interested were represented, the most notable outcome was the extension to all nations of " the most-favoured nation treatment," hitherto confined to France and Britain. The treaty was signed by all the Western European

* Oppenheim, " International Law," vol. ii., p. 71. ⁻

Powers and by the United States.   Far
more explicit, however, were the provisions
for equality of economic opportunity furnished by the Act of Algeçiras.   It provided
not only for equality of trade, but for strict
impartiality in loans and investments obtained from foreign countries.   Still more
important, the advantage of international
over purely national control is shown in the
provisions made for protecting the legitimate
rights of the backward country which is the
object of economic penetration.

As to the public services and the construction of public works, the Act declared that
in no case should the rights of the " State
over the public services of the Sheereefian
Empire be alienated for the benefit of
private interests."   If the Moorish Government had recourse to foreign capital or
industries in connection with the public
services or public works, the Powers under-
took to see that " the control of the State
over such large undertakings of public interest remain intact "; tenders, " without

respect of nationality," should regulate all
orders for public works or the furnishing of
supplies ; no specification for orders should
contain either " explicitly or implicitly any
condition or provision of a nature to violate
the principle of free competition or to place
the competitors of one nationality at a dis-
advantage as against the competitors of
another " ; "regulations as to contracts
should be drawn up by the Moorish
Government and the Diplomatic Body at
Tangier."*

This Agreement presents an excellent
model for the larger policy of the Open
Door, in defining the economic relations of
the Governments and peoples of advanced
towards backward countries. If all backward
countries, whether under the political control
of some European or other " advanced "
State or still politically independent, were
formally recognized by Conventions of
the civilized Powers as similarly open to

* "Ten Years of Secret Diplomacy," by E. D. Morel,
p. 31.

the trading and investing members of all countries on a basis of economic equality, with adequate mutual guarantees for the enforcement of the treaty obligations, the greatest step towards lasting and universal peace would have been taken.

It would need, however, to be supplemented and supported by other steps in order to achieve the full policy of equality of economic opportunity and to safeguard the interests of the inhabitants of backward areas thus brought within the area of economic internationalism. The substance of the Open Door policy may be stated in the following four proposals, which, in order to be effective, should be incorporated in a general Treaty or Convention signed by all the Powers:

1. Freedom of access for traders and goods of all nations to trade routes by land, river, canal, or sea, including the use of rail terminals, ports and coaling-stations, police protection and other facilities, upon terms of equality. Countries like Servia or Poland must not be at the mercy of possibly hostile

neighbours for commercial access to the out-side world. The export of wheat from Russia and Roumania must not be impeded in the future, as often in the past, by the closing of the Dardanelles. No Power must hold the keys of the Mediterranean or the Pacific. The Panama and Kiel Canals must be placed on the same basis of free use as the Suez Canal. No Power must reserve the right to close trade-gates at any time to traders of other nations.

2. Equal admission to markets and other trading facilities to be accorded by all Powers to foreign traders in all their dependencies.

This provision (an extension of the existing British practice) would leave it open to the Powers to retain tariff and other protection for their home markets. It would simply preclude them from extending the area of Protection to colonies, protectorates, and spheres of influence. Self-governing colonies, already possessing and exercising full control over their commercial and fiscal policy, would also be excluded from this stipulation.

3. Equal opportunities for the investment of capital in every form of business enter-prise and for full legal protection of all property for members of all nations in the dependencies of other nations.

4. The establishment of International

Commissions to secure equality of treatment for the commerce, investments and other property interests, of the subjects of the treaty Powers, in all backward or undeveloped countries not under the political control of any Power. Such Commissions might by concerted action exercise a restrictive control over the nature of the trade with "lower races," precluding, for example, the importation of arms or alcoholic liquors. They might also exercise a supervising authority over the loans and investments made by financiers to the Governments or private persons in these backward countries, and over the methods of business exploitation employed by the agents of the investing companies.

Whether these Commissions should endeavour to interpret "equality of opportunity" by some process of apportioning special spheres of interest and enterprise to the members of the several Powers, or whether they should encourage direct co-operation in the work of investment and development between business men of different nations, is a question into which I need not enter here. But readers may be reminded that control by International Commission is no untried method of regulating the diverse and conflicting interests of States. Four International Commissions have been instituted for dealing with questions of navigation, on the Danube, the Congo, and the Suez Canal. Three International Commissions have concerned themselves with questions of sanitation on the Lower Danube, at Constantinople, and at Alexandria. Three others are concerned with the interest of foreign creditors in Turkey, Egypt, and Greece, while a permanent Commission relating to sugar bounties was set up in 1902 by the Brussels Convention.

Why should not some such machinery by Commission be extended and endowed with adequate administrative powers, so as to form the nucleus of an efficient international Government regulating those economic relations between the advanced and backward peoples which are the most dangerous causes of dispute between modern Governments?

Taken in conjunction with the other applications of the Open Door, this direct endeavour to give a positive construction to the principle of equality of opportunity would seem to be the most feasible and efficacious way of dealing with the gravest practical problem of our time.*

This policy I present as the true alternative to the reactionary policy of economic nationalism urged by our New Protectionists in the name of defence. The true defence, the only possible security against future wars, is to extend and strengthen the bonds of economic and human intercourse between members of all nations, to remove the causes of economic antagonism which have hitherto bred dissension, and to substitute conditions of fair competition and fruitful co-operation. The issue is indeed a grave one. Are we to aim at breaking up the economic world into self-contained

* A vigorous and well-informed advocacy of International Commissions is contained in Mr. Lippmann's "The Stakes of Diplomacy" (Henry Holt and Co.).

nations, or groups of nations, not indifferent
but actively hostile to one another in all
parts of the earth, and incessantly engaged
in fighting one another by tariffs, boycotts,
Navigation Acts, and every weapon and
barrier they can command, reducing the
total productivity of the earth, increasing
the difficulties of transport and commerce,
and enforcing the application of an ever-
growing proportion of each nation's wealth
to war preparations which ever tend to fulfil
the fearful purpose for which they are designed?   Or are we to trust to the salutary
effects of a Free Trade which has not yet
been adequately tried, and to the extension
of its principles to the new conditions of
international intercourse by the establishment of public international control and
guarantees?   Place the risks and the difficulties of this latter policy as high as you
choose, they fall immeasurably short of
those to which the former policy exposes
this nation and the world.   The path of
safety, as of opulence, lies in the forward

movement towards economic internationalism, not in a reversion towards a national
economy which for a country with our past
and present is impracticable, and, were it
practicable, would be none the less a be-
trayal of civilization for ourselves and for
humanity.

Article 10

POLITICAL SCIENCE
QUARTERLY

WHY THE WAR CAME AS A SURPRISE

THE war fell upon us in the summer of 1914 as a terrible surprise. Hardly anybody had believed in its coming. A handful of dismal pacifists in the different countries, pointing to the growth of armaments, had uttered their vaticinations. Little knots of ardent militarists with their business companions, bent upon increased preparedness, talked confidently of the inevitable day, forgetting to reconcile their prediction with the preventive virtues which they attributed to warlike preparations. But few even of these extremists of either group seriously believed that war was imminent. There were, no doubt, a few in Germany and elsewhere who in the latter days believed in war because they had contrived it and resolved upon it. But for our immediate purposes these may stand out of the account.

It is this general surprise and the ignorance to which it testifies that demand explanation. How came it about that people of every grade of knowledge and intelligence were so utterly blind to the real state of the world in the spring of 1914? The unthinking have chosen to compare the event with some catastrophe of nature or to dramatize it as a desperate crime of the rulers of a single nation. But though there is an element of truth in both of these explanations, neither affords reasonable satisfaction. For to make such a catastrophe or such a crime seem possible, the whole world and the people in it must have been greatly different from what we thought them. Yet there was not one of the concrete issues which carried the seeds of strife, not one of the deep-seated divergencies of policy, nor one of the fierce suspicions, hates, ambitions and cupidities in which danger might lurk, that was not exposed to innumerable watchful eyes. There was no lack of knowledge of the danger areas or of the dangers which they held. But in spite of all this knowledge the general sense of security was not seriously shaken. It was as in the days of Noah but without the pretext the people then had for not listening to the warnings of a senile croaker.

This false sense of security was the product of a habitual misvaluation of the contentious forces and the checks upon them. The former were gravely underestimated, while heavily inflated value was given to the latter. Both errors are attributable to a single cause, an excessive appreciation of men's moral and rational attainments and of the part they actually play in the guidance of individual and collective conduct. The doctrine of the perfectability of man implicit in every higher religion, coupled with a faith in the power of enlightened self-interest to accomplish swift reforms in the fabric of human society, lay at the root of all the liberal revolutionary movements of the half century that followed the French Revolution. The world was so constituted that everyone, in striving to preserve his own life and to promote his own happiness, was impelled along lines of conduct that conduced to the welfare of others. But he was also a social being in feeling and will, capable of conscious effort for the good of others and taking pleasure in every task of mutual aid. Sometimes the stress was laid upon enlightened selfishness, sometimes upon the social emotions. In either case, human relations were believed to be grounded in rationality.

The greatest moral discovery of the nineteenth century, that man belonged body and soul to the natural world, and that the whole of his life and conduct was subject to the reign of law, had profound reactions upon social thought and policy, especially in the spheres of statecraft and industry. Though the immediate philosophic fruit of this discovery was determinism, this rational creed had nothing in common with the paralyzing fatalism charged against it by orthodox critics. On the contrary it suffered at the hands of its chief exponents from an excessive faith in the power of man to mould his destiny, adapting and creating institutions for his wholesome needs and desires with an ease and a celerity that made light of the human heritage of habits and attachments.   It is impossible to follow the various currents of reforming zeal from Godwin, Shelley and the youthful Coleridge, through the more definite proposals and experiments of Bentham, Owen, John Stuart Mill and their philosophic-radical, chartist and social followers, without being confronted by a belief in man's power to be the arbiter of his fate quite staggering in the measure of its confidence.   Bentham's contempt for history was indeed characteristic of his liberalism, which demanded a liberation as complete as possible from all trammels of the past.   Though commonly coupled with repudiation of existing religious dogmas, this nineteenth-century rationalism conducted itself with the fervor of religious zeal.

The faith in reason rested upon two assumptions.   First, that reason was by right and in fact the supreme arbiter in human conduct; and second, that a complete harmony of human relations was discoverable and attainable by getting reason to prevail in individual and national affairs.   " Getting reason to prevail " meant opening wide the portals to knowledge and removing the positive barriers of law, traditions, prejudice and passion which blocked the play of enlightened self-interest.   This faith, penetrating alike the individualism of Bentham and the socialism of Owen, may be regarded as a practical mysticism, deriving its nourishment partly from the philosophy of the Revolution, partly from the miraculous technology of the new machine industry.   If applied reason can so immensely and so rapidly enlarge the bounds of material productivity, cannot the same power beneficially transform the entire structure of human society?   Abundant wealth, equitably distributed among the producers by the operation of inevitable laws, would form the material basis of a new moral world.   A free, instructed people would cooperate in a hundred ways for their mutual advantage.   Though one of these ways would be the state, political democracy was not the chief concern.   For in the rational world the coercive arm of society would have

little scope.   The functions of the state were to be purely defensive, directed to prevent the interference of one person with
another within the national limits and of one nation with another in the wider world of states and governments.   The reasonable will of individual citizens would preserve harmony and
promote social progress within the several nations and in the
wider sphere of humanity, if only free play were secured for it.
The state was conceived of as an essentially artificial and repres-
sive instrument whose operation should be kept at a minimum.
Hence it came about that the early socialistic proposals commonly gave the state the go-by and based themselves upon the
purely voluntary association of individual citizens.   This limited
conception of the state imparted a certain unsubstantiality to
the radical and chartist agitations for an extended franchise and
other instruments of political democracy.   These agitations
were rather the indices of popular discontents, rooted in the
miserable social-economic conditions of the working classes,
than a firm and natural expression of the popular will seeking
incorporation in the state.   That is why these agitations were
dissipated in the mid-nineteenth century by small political concessions floated on the rising tide of a trade prosperity which
gave relief and hope to the organizing artisan classes that represented the lower strata of political consciousness.

There was in the mid-century no clear recognition anywhere,
save in a few eccentric or disordered brains, of the necessity
and feasibility of converting and enlarging the machinery of
government into a means of so controlling industry and distributing its fruits as to secure a reasonable livelihood for all
and to remedy the palpable injustices in the apportionment of
this world's goods.   There had been plenty of shrewd and
trenchant exposures of the abuses of land ownership and of the
factory system with their related evils of unemployment, sweating wages, oppression of child life, unsanitary housing, poor
law degradation and the like.   But though the state was looked
to for supplying certain minor safeguards, the liberative tide
was still in the ascendant, and the free play of enlightened self-
interest in competitive industry was still the animating faith of
the friends of popular progress.

This typical middle-class sentimental rationalism long succeeded in diverting popular self-government from all thoughts or plans of economic democracy. Though Mazzini, as early as the late thirties, had made his brilliant exposure of the futility of a political revolution which left the keys of industrial masterhood in the hands of a new capitalistic oligarchy, neither the mind nor the circumstances of any great people were ripe for its reception. The nationalistic spirit, guided by bourgeois leaders and ambitions, was a dominant factor in the continental revolutions of the mid-century, and the economic communism which flared up for a brief period in the large French cities was in reality little more than an ill-prepared by-product of a cooperative spirit which found more immediately profitable expression in trade-union and other non-political spheres of activity. The early socialism, alike of Owen and of the Christian Socialists of the next generation, must properly rank as a variant of this bourgeois rationalism, inspired with a larger measure of social compunction and with a more conscious reliance upon the forces of human comradeship. The deep sentimentalism in which men like Kingsley and Maurice steeped their teaching should not hide this essential truth. So long as the firm faith in a natural harmony of interests, personal and national, operating either through competition or the private cooperation of individuals, continued to be the prevailing creed of social reformers, there was little hope of effective organic reform. For neither the harder rationalism of the Manchester School nor the softer of the early socialism was capable of yielding a nutritious and stimulating gospel to the people. Its essential defects were two. The first was this open and persistent cleavage between political and industrial advancement, serving to enfeeble the democratic movement by removing from its scope the most vital and appealing issues. The second was the naively middle-class character of the politics and economics. In national and still more in local politics the new well-to-do business classes with their professional retinue were obtrusively dominant in all issues which touched either their pockets or their class pride. Their dominance was not seriously impaired by the several extensions of the franchise succeeding the Reform Act of 1832, which first put them in the saddle. Their superior wealth, control over employment, dominant personality, prestige and organizing power kept in their hands the levers of politics and enabled them with no great difficulty to influence and manipulate the widening working-class electorate. They continued to use this power so as to encourage the belief that substantial equality of opportunity existed and that personal character was everywhere an assured road to success and prosperity, while they prolonged the career of liberalism by concentrating the party struggle on numerous separate little liberative missions, conducted slowly and piecemeal, thus staving off the bigger organic reforms that were emerging in the new radicalism of the later half-century.

It was not a conscious statecraft, but the instinctive self-defence of the bourgeois politician. A free scope for private competitive enterprise alike in domestic, industrial and foreign trade, with such personal liberties and opportunities of education, movement, choice of trade, thrift and comfort for the workers as would keep them industrious and contented with their lot and with the economic and political leadership of the employing middle classes—such was the prevailing thought of the men who boasted themselves the backbone of the country. It was not necessary or desirable to make it into a theory or a system. For that process was rather a hindrance than an aid to practice. Though able exponents of the theory presented themselves, the ruling bourgeoisie assimilated only fragments of the teaching. From their authoritative economists they took a few convenient dogmas, such as the law of rent and the wage fund, for weapons in their encounters with land owners, trade unions and meddling philanthropists. Their political philosophers and lawyers furnished a little rhetoric about freedom of contract, personal rights and the limits of legislative and administrative government, with which they eked out a confined but serviceable policy for their dealings with the state. The larger complexity of the philosophic radicalism never entered the brains or hearts of these hard practical men who knew what they wanted and meant to get it. Even the simpler gospel of Cobden, with its glow of moral fervor, had too much theory in it to prove acceptable to more than a little handful. His lamentations over the desertion of his principles of cosmopolitanism by the majority of those who heard him gladly when he led them to cheap food and prosperous export trade, are an instructive testimony to the disinclination of the new dominant class for any coherent social thinking. The fate of the socialistic doctrines that later in the century displaced the mid-Victorian individualism was very similar. Neither the proletarian brand which German revolutionists had manufactured from the materials exported from this country and reexported a generation later, nor the superior academic brand compounded of Rousseau, Hegel and T. H. Green, which, mixed with Jevonian economics, nourished the young lions of Fabianism, found any wide or deep acceptance among any class of our people. This, of course, does not imply that they were negligible as impelling or directive forces in the political and economic movements of the age. For though ideologists vastly overrate the general influence of their ideas and *isms* in moulding human affairs, the cumulative value of the particular thoughts and sentiments and even formulas which they suggest to politicians, business men and practical reformers, has been considerable even in England, the country least susceptible to the direct and conscious guidance of ideas. What practical men take from theorists in Britain is pointers along roads that circumstances have already opened up for possible advance. Just as the theorizing of Adam Smith and Ricardo, working through the agitation of the anti-corn law leaguers, drove Peel and his politicians into a piecemeal free trade, so the new thinking on the positive functions of government led the municipal reformers of the eighties and nineties to tackle with more confidence their gas-and-water-socialism and still later helped to remove some obstinate barriers to the development of national services for health, education and insurance.

Although there is a natural tendency just now to overstress every antithesis between our ways and those of Germany, it cannot be denied that a wide difference has existed in the operative force of theories and systems in the two countries. The disposition and the habit of working from thought-out purposes

through plans to concrete arrangements is justly cited as the
peculiar quality of Prussian social craft, from the time at least
of Stein and Humboldt onward.   Nor is it by any means confined to high politics.   The contrast with our ways is even
more striking in the subsidiary realms of education, transport,
credit, town planning, insurance and industrial structure.   Compare the development of our so-called railway system, our
banking, the unregulated spread of our great cities or the
emergence of our business combines with those of Germany.
Our way has been that of groping empiricism, not merely not
believing in theories and preconcerted plans but even disbe-
lieving in them.   There may at first sight seem to be an incon-
sistency between this view of our national way of going on and
the rationalistic error which we found at the root of our failure
to understand the state of the world in 1914.   The contradiction, however, is only apparent, for at the root of our refusal
to think things out in advance, to arrange consciously the forces
adequate to attain a clearly conceived end, is a sort of half
belief and half feeling that it doesn't pay to think things out.
Our practice of tackling difficulties when they come, improvis-
ing ways of overcoming them, and in general of muddling
through, we really hold to be a sound policy.   Nor is this
judgment or sentiment sheer mental inertia or mere inability
to think straight or far.   It drives down to that rationalism
which I have identified with practical mysticism in a conviction
of the existence of some order in human affairs along the tide
of which we may reasonably allow ourselves to float with confidence that somehow we shall reach the haven where we would
be.   We are opportunists on principle.   That principle implies
belief in a generally favorable drift or tendency, or even a
Providence upon which we may rely to see us through and
which dispenses with the obligation to practice much fore-
thought.   In America this is called the doctrine of manifest
destiny.   But we feel that even to make a conscious doctrine
of it interferes with its spontaneity.   The great historical example of this way of life is our empire, rightly described as
built up in " a fit of absence of mind."   To Teutonic statecraft
such a statement ranks as sheer hypocrisy, but none the less it

is the truth. Individual builders there have been and bits of personal planning, but never has the edifice of empire presented itself as an object of policy or even of desire to our government or people. Its general purpose can be found only in terms of drift or tendency. It will no doubt be urged that irrationalism is a more appropriate term than rationalism to describe this state of mind. But my point is that the state of mind implies the existence of some immanent reason in history working toward harmony and justifying optimism. Reason in the nature of things happily dispenses with the painful toil of clear individual thinking.

These general reflections may help to explain the universal surprise at the collapse of our world in 1914. For whether we regard the theorizing few or the many content with practice, we find no perception of the formidable nature of the antagonisms which for several generations had been gathering strength for open conflict. Even the historical commentators of today, as they survey and group into general movements the large happenings of the nineteenth century, often exhibit the same blindness which I have imputed to the current theorists. The smooth bourgeois optimism which characterised the liberal thinkers of the mid-century in their championship of nationalism, parliamentary institutions, broad franchise, free trade, capitalistic industry and internationalism, is discernible in the present-day interpreters of these movements. Take for example that widest stream of political events in Europe designated as the movement for national self-government. Historians distinguish its two currents or impulses, one making for national unity or government, the nation state in its completeness, and another seeking to establish democratic rule within the state. Correct in regarding this common flow and tendency of events as of profound significance, they have usually over-valued the achievements. On the one hand, they have taken too formal a view of the liberative processes with which they deal, and, on the other, they have failed to appreciate the flaws in the working of the so-called democratic institutions.

The reign of machinery, the outward and visible sign of nineteenth-century progress, has annexed our very minds and processes of thinking. Mechanical metaphors have secretly imposed themselves upon our politics and squeezed out humanity. That willing communion of intelligence which should constitute a party has become in name and in substance a " machine "; politics are "engineered ", and divergent interests are reconciled by " balance of power ". I should be far from describing the great nationalist movement of the nineteenth century as mechanical. It was the product of passionate enthusiasms as well as of the play of reasonable interests. The struggle for liberation on the part of subject nationalities and for unification in the place of division broke out in a dozen different quarters during the first half of the century, and the two following decades saw the movement not indeed completed, but brought to a long halt in which splendid successes were recorded. In some cases, as in Germany and to a less extent in Italy, dynastic, military, fiscal and transport considerations were powerful propellers toward unification. But everywhere a genuinely national sentiment, based on a varying blend of racial, religious, linguistic and territorial community, gave force and nourishment to the new national structure. Its liberative and self-realizing virtues were not garnered in Europe alone. The foundations of the nationhood of our great oversea dominions were laid in the colonial policy of this epoch, while the breaking-away of the Spanish-American colonies from their European attachment caused a great expansion of national self-government in the new world. But nationalism, regarded as the spirit and the practice of racial and territorial autonomy, has borne an exceedingly precarious relation to democracy. It has been consistent with the tyrannous domination of a dynasty, a caste or class, within the area of the nation. Indeed at all times the spirit of nationality has been subject to exploitation by a dominant class for the suppression of internal discontents and the defence of privileges. Stein, Hardenburg, Bismarck and Treitschke used the enthusiasm of nationalism to fasten the fetters of a dominant Prussian caste upon the Germanic peoples. The struggles for the maintenance of the recovery of Polish and Hungarian national independence were directed by the ruling ambitions of an oppressive racial and economic oligarchy.

Professor Ramsay Muir, in his interesting study of the relations between nationality and self-government in the nineteenth century, greatly overstrains the actual association of the movements. If self-government signifies, as it should, the direct participation of the whole people in its government, though some temporal coincidence appears, there is as much antagonism as sympathy in the actual operation of the two tendencies in modern history. Nationalism is used as often to avert as to foster democracy. For although the appeal to the racial unity and common spirit of a people for the assertion of its integrity and independence must indisputably tend to arouse in the common people a dignity and a desire to have a voice in public affairs, the leadership and prestige of military or political champions in the struggle may often suffice to foster or extort a servile consent of the governed as a feeble substitute for democracy. Indeed, it is precisely on this negative attribute that Professor Muir relies when he insists that " the land-owning aristocracy of the eighteenth century ruled Britain by consent " and that in Britain, France and Belgium after 1830, the " effective popular control of a government was henceforth solidly established." But the failure of a subject people or a subject class to revolt against its rulers is no true consent. Nor does the irregular connection between nationality and parliamentary government go far toward identifying nationalism with democracy as the typical achievement in the politics of the nineteenth century. None of the extensions of the franchise in Britain in the nineteenth century secured full and effective self-government for the people or even for the enlarged electorate regarded as representative of the people. Historians and politicians alike have deceived themselves and others by a grave over-valuation of mere electoral machinery. Neither by the popularization of the franchise nor by the less formal operation of public opinion has the reality of democratic government been secured. The power of the aristo-plutocracy, somewhat changed in composition and demanding more cunning and discretion for its successful operation, still stands substantially unimpaired in Britain, France and America. Through the organs of public opinion the governing few still pump down their will upon the electorate, to draw it up again with the formal endorsement of an unreal general will or consent of the governed.

The conviction that political security and progress are made effective by the union of national independence and representative government rests upon a totally defective analysis, which was responsible in no small measure for the failure to forecast and to prevent the collapse of 1914. The nature of the flaw in this reasoning is slow to become apparent to the middle-class intelligence necessarily approaching public affairs with the prepossessions of its class. We can best discover it by turning once more to the defects of nationalism. The first we have already indicated, *viz.*, the masking of the interests or ambitions of a ruling, owning, class or caste in the national movement. Nationalism is often internally oppressive. But a second vice bred of struggle and the intensity of self-realization is an exclusiveness which easily lends itself to fiscal or military policies of national defence, through which dangerous separatist interests are fostered within the national state. The spirit of nationalism, stimulated by the struggle for independence, easily becomes so self-centered as to make its devotees reckless of the vital interests of the entire outside world. To Irish Nationalists, Czeckoslovaks or Poles, this vast world struggle has been apt to figure merely or mainly as their great opportunity for the achievement of a national aim to which they are willing to sacrifice without a qualm the lives, property and rights of all other peoples. This absorbing passion, like others, is exploited for various ends and is the spiritual sustenance of the protectionism that always brings grist to the commercial mill. But there is a third defect of nationalism, of the nature of excess. It may become inflated and express itself in political and territorial aggrandizement. Imperialism is nationalism run riot and turned from self-possession to aggression. No modern nation can pursue a policy of isolation. It must have foreign relations, and its foreign policy may become " spirited ", passing rashly into schemes of conquest and annexation.

These three perversions of nationalism, the oppressive, the exclusive and the aggressive, are all grounded in the domination of a nation by a predominant class or set of interests. This class power is rooted often in traditional prestige, but this prestige itself rests upon solid economic supports. Landlordism and serfdom, capitalism and wagedom, moneylending and indebtedness—such have been the distinctive cleavages which have so often made a mockery of the boasted national freedom.

If we turn from this survey of nineteenth-century nationalism to a consideration of the democratic movement with which it has been associated, we discover that "democracy" is vitiated by the same defects. It either signifies parliamentarism upon an utterly inadequate franchise, by which the majority of the governed have no electoral voice, or else the formal government by the people is a machine controlled for all essential purposes by small powerful groups and interests. Political democracy based upon economic equality is as yet an unattained ideal.

The liberal political philosophy of the Victorian era failed entirely to comprehend this vital flaw in the movement of nationalism and democracy. That failure was chiefly caused by its underlying assumption that politics and business are independent spheres. According to this view it was as illicit for business interests to handle politics as for government to encroach upon business interests. Such interference from either side appeared unnecessary and injurious. It was not perceived that the evolution of modern industry, commerce and finance had two important bearings upon politics. In the first place, it impelled business interests to exercise political pressure upon government for tariff aids, lucrative public contracts and favorable access to foreign markets and areas of development. Secondly, it evoked a growing demand for the protection of weaker industries, the workers and the consuming public, from the oppressive power of strong corporations and combinations which in many of the essential trades were displacing competition.

In other words, history was playing havoc with the economic harmonies upon which Bastiat and Cobden relied for the peaceful and fruitful cooperation of capital and labor within the nation and of commerce between the different countries of the world. Cobden valiantly assailed the militarism, protectionism and imperialism of his day and recognized their affinity of spirit and certain of their common business aims, but without any full perception of their economic taproot or of the rapid domination over foreign policy which they were soon destined to attain. The grave social-economic problems which have lately loomed so large in the statecraft of every country lay then unrecognized. Throughout the long public career of two such genuinely liberal statesmen as Cobden and Gladstone neither evinced the slightest recognition that the state had any interest or obligation in respect of the health and housing, the wages, hours and tenure of employment, the settlement of issues between capital and labor, or in any drastic reforms of our feudal land system. So far as they recognized these economic grievances at all, they deemed individual or privately-associated effort to be the proper and adequate mode of redress. Where government was called upon to intervene for liberative or constructive work, the superficiality of its treatment showed a quite abysmal ignorance of social structure. A generation in which the Artisans Dwelling Act of 1875, the Ground Game and Small Holdings Act of the early eighties and the factory acts of 1870 and 1878 ranked as serious contributions to a new social policy, is self-condemned for utter incapacity to see, much less to solve, the social problem. Such statecraft failed to perceive that the new conditions of modern capitalist trade and finance had poisoned the policies of nationality and democratic self-government and were breeding antagonisms that would bring class war within each nation and international war in its train.

Not until the eighties did these antagonisms begin to become evident to those with eyes to see. During the period from 1850 to 1880 Britain still remained so far ahead of other countries in her industrial development, her foreign trade, her shipping and her finance, that she entertained no fears of serious rivalry. Though our markets and those of our world-wide empire were formally open upon equal terms to foreign merchants, our traders held the field, and British enterprise and capital met little competition in European markets or in loans for the great railroad development in North and South America. Not until the industrial countries of the Continent had reconstituted their industries upon British models and had furnished themselves with steam transport, while the United States, recovered from the Civil War, was advancing rapidly along the same road, was any check put upon the optimism which held that England was designed by Providence to be the abiding workshop of the world. Throughout the mid-Victorian era our economists and social prophets, with a few exceptions, were satisfied with a national prosperity and progress which enriched business classes, while the level of comfort among the skilled artisans showed a considerable and fairly constant rise.

Internally, the economic harmony appeared, at any rate to well-to-do observers, to be justified by events. Externally, there seemed no reason for suspecting any gathering conflict from the fact that one great nation after another was entering upon the path of industrial capitalism. Why should the rising productivity and trade of Germany, the United States and other developing nations, be any source of enmity or injury to us? The economic harmonies were clear in their insistence that free intercourse would bring about an international division of labor as profitable to all the participating nations as the similar division of labor within each nation was to its individual members. It was impossible for the world to produce too much wealth or to produce it too rapidly for the satisfaction of the expanding wants of its customers. Foolish persons prated of over-production and pointed to recurrent periods of trade depression and unemployment. But the harmonists saw nothing in these phenomena but such friction, miscalculation and maladjustment as were involved in the processes of structural change and the elasticity of markets. As a noted economist of the eighties put it, "the modern system of industry will not work without a margin of unemployment."

All the same, several notable occurrences in the eighties ruffled the complacency of mid-Victorian optimism. One was the revelation of the massed poverty and degradation of the slum-dwellers in our towns and the searchlight turned upon working-class conditions in this and other lands by the competing criticisms of Henry George and the newly formed Socialist organizations. The second was the rise in the United States of those trusts and other formidable combinations, which emerged as the culmination and the cancellation of that competition upon which the harmonists relied for the salutary operation of their economic laws. The third did not assume at first sight an economic face. It was the testimony to competing imperialism furnished by the Berlin Conference for the partition of Central Africa. This was the first intimation to the world of a new rivalry the true nature of which lay long concealed under the garb of foreign policy and was at the time by no means plain to the statesmen who were its executants.

Imperialism is not, indeed, a simple policy with a single motive. It is compact of political ambition, military adventure, philanthropic and missionary enterprise and sheer expansionism, partly for settlement, partly for power, partly for legitimate and materially gainful trade. But more and more, as the white man's world has been occupied and colonized, the aggrandizing instincts have turned to those tropical and subtropical countries where genuine white colonization is impossible and where rich natural resources and submissive backward peoples present the opportunity of a new and distinctively economic empire.

Since the compelling pressure for this greed of empire has been the main source of the growing discord in the modern world, it is of the utmost importance to understand how the discord rises and to see its organic relation to the class war within the several nations which has grown contemporaneously with it. If modern industrial society were closely conformable to the economic harmonies, the mobility and competition of capital and business ability would ensure that no larger share of the product should be obtained by the owners of those productive agents than served to promote their usual growth and efficiency, and that the surplus of the fruits of industry should pass to the general body of the working population in their capacity of wage earners and consumers, through the instrumentality of high wages and low prices. Combinations of workers would be needless and mischievous, for they could not increase the aggregate that would fall to labor, and the gains they might secure for stronger groups of workers would be at the expense of the weaker sections. It was to the interest of labor that capital and business ability should be well remunerated, in order that the increase of savings and of the wage fund should be as large as possible, and that the arts of invention and business enterprise should be stimulated to the utmost. For labor was the residuary legatee of this fruitful cooperation. It was, again, a manifest impossibility that production should outstrip consumption, for somebody had a lien upon everything that was produced, and the wants of men were illimitable. Thus effective demand must keep pace with every increase of supply. The notion that members of the same trade were hostile competitors, in the sense that there was not enough market to go round, and that, if some sold their goods, others would fail to sell, seemed a palpable absurdity.

Yet it was precisely these impossibilities and absurdities that asserted themselves as dominant facts in the operation of modern capitalist business. Every business man knew from experience that a chronic tendency to produce more goods than could profitably be sold prevailed over large fields of industry, that the wheels of industry had frequently and for long periods to be slowed down in order to prevent over-production, and that more and more work, money, force and skill had to be put into the selling as distinguished from the productive side of business. Every instructed worker knew that wealth was not in fact distributed in accordance with the economic harmonies, that much of it stuck in the form of rent and other unearned or excessive payments for well-placed capital and brains, and that the great gains of the technical improvements did not come down to "the residual legatee". Where free competition survived, it became cut-throat, leading to unremunerative prices, congested markets and frequent stoppages; when effective combination took its place, restricted output and regulated prices operated both in restraint of production and in the emergence of monopoly. Put otherwise, the weaker bargaining power of labor, pitted against the superior material resources, organization, knowledge and other strategic advantages of the land-owning, capitalistic and entrepreneur classes, left the former with an effective demand for commodities too small to purchase the products of the machine industries as fast as these were capable of providing them. The habitual under-consumption of the workers, due to the massing of unearned or excessive income in the hands of the master classes, has been the plainest testimony to the reality of that antagonism of interests within each nation which is dramatized as "class war". No smooth talk about the real identity of interests between capital and labor disposes of the issue. A real identity does exist within certain limits. It does not pay capitalists, employers, landowners or other strong bargainers to drive down wages below the level of efficiency. Nor does it pay labor, even should it possess the power, to force down "profits" below what is required, under the existing arrangements, to maintain a good flow of capital and technical and business ability into a trade. But wherever the state of trade is such as to yield a return more than enough to cover these minimum provisions, the surplus is a real "bone of contention" and lies entirely outside the economic harmonies. It goes to the stronger party as the spoils of actual or potential class war. Strikes and lockouts are not the wholly irrational and wasteful actions they appear at first sight. In default of any more reasonable or equitable way of distributing the surplus among the claimants, they rank as a natural and necessary process. However much we may deplore class war, it is to this extent a reality and does testify to an existing class antagonism inside our social-economic system.

I have already explained by implication how this inherent antagonism of classes contains the seeds of the wider antagonism of states and governments. The maldistribution of wealth, which keeps the consuming power of the people persistently below the producing power of machine industry, impels the controllers of that industry to direct more and more of their energy to securing foreign markets to take the goods they cannot sell at home and to prevent producers in other countries, confronted with the same necessity, from entering their home market. Here is a simultaneous drive for governmental aid: first, in protecting the home market from the invasion of foreign goods; secondly, in inducing or coercing the governments of foreign countries to admit our goods into their market on more favorable terms than those of other competing countries. Hence arise three policies, all pregnant with international antagonism. The protection, adopted primarily in order to secure home trade and keep out the foreigner, is a constant breeder of dissension among peoples and governments. Its secondary effect, to assist strong combinations within a country to stifle free competition and by imposing high prices to increase the volume of surplus profit, further aggravates the maldistribution of the national income, which we recognize as the mother of discord. For this increased surplus means a further restriction of internal consumption and a corresponding pressure for enlarged foreign outlets. More and more must the capitalist classes in each industrially advanced country press their governments for protection at home and a powerful bagman's policy abroad.

Protection, however, is only the first plank in this platform. The second is diplomatic and other pressure brought to bear on weaker states for trading privileges or special spheres of commercial interests, as in China and Persia, or for the enforcement of debt payment or other business arrangements in which private traders or investors demand redress for injuries. This last consideration introduces the third and by far the most important cause of international discord. The surplus income under modern capitalism, it must be recognized, cannot be absorbed in extending the productive machinery needed to supply our home markets. Nor can it find full remunerative occupation in the supply of foreign markets, either under the condition of free competition with exporters from other countries or by such trading privileges as those to which we have alluded. An increasing proportion of that surplus income must be permanently invested in other countries. This has been the most important factor in the economic and political transformation of the world during the last generation. Under the direction of skilled financiers an increasing flow of surplus or savings has gone about the world, knocking at every door of profitable investment and using governmental pressure wherever it was necessary. Special railway, mining or land concessions, loans pressed upon state governments or municipalities or in backward countries upon kinglets or tribal chiefs, the pegging out of permanently profitable stakes in foreign lands—these methods have been employed by strong business syndicates everywhere with more or less support from their government. Such areas, at first penetrated by private business enterprise, soon acquire a political significance, which grows along a sliding scale of slippery language from " spheres of legitimate aspiration " to " spheres of influence ", protectorates and colonial possessions. Now, just as there are not enough home markets for goods or capital to take up the trade " surplus ", so there is found to be not enough world market for the growing pressure of world capital seeking these outside areas of investment and the markets which go with them. More and more this pressure of financiers for profitable foreign fields has played in with the political ambitions of statesmen to make the inflammatory composition of modern imperialism. This imperialism is thus seen to be the close congener of the capitalism and protectionism that are the roots of class antagonism within the several nations. While it nourishes jealousies, suspicions and hostilities between nations, it also strengthens the master classes in every nation by forging the joint political and economic weapons of protection and militarism and crossing and so confusing the class antagonism by masquerading as " nationalism ". Quite plainly the imperialist or capitalist says to the worker: " Come in with us in our great imperialistic exploitation of the world. This is the only way of securing the large, expanding and remunerative markets necessary to furnish full, regular employment at high wages. Come in with us and share an illimitable surplus, got not from under-paying you but out of the untapped resources of the tropics worked for our joint benefit by the lower races." This invitation to wholesale parasitism is openly flaunted by such bodies as the Imperial Development Resources Committee and is more timidly suggested in various new projects for harmonizing the interests of capital and labor on the basis of the development of capitalistic combinations. Were it successful, it would do nothing to heal the discord either between capital and labor in this country or between the divergent interests of capitalist groups in the several countries. Nay, even if it were extended by some international concert of western capitalist powers to a more or less complete control of the tropics, it would only enlarge the area of discord by arraying the ruling nations of the world against the lower races whom they had set to grind out wealth to be taken for the masters' consumption.

I must not, however, carry further at this stage this speculative glance into the possible future. For what concerns us here is to understand the sources of the blindness which caused the war to break upon us as a horrible surprise. I desire here to show that this blindness lay in a deep-seated misapprehension of the dominant movements of the century and particularly of the latest outcomes of perverted nationalism and capitalism in their joint reactions upon foreign relations.

We have seen these two dominant forces emerging and moulding the course of actual events. Nationalism and capitalism in secret conjunction produced independent, armed and opposed powers within each country, claiming and wielding a paramountcy, political, social and economic, within the nation and working for further expansion outside. This competition of what may fairly be called capitalist states, evolving modern forms of militarism and protectionism, laid the powder trains. The dramatic antithesis of aggressive autocracies and pacific democracies in recent history is false, and the failure to discern this falsehood explains the great surprise. Nowhere had the conditions of a pacific democracy been established. Everywhere an inflamed and aggrandizing nationalism had placed the growing powers of an absolute state (absolute alike in its demands upon its citizens and in its attitude to other states) at the disposal of powerful oligarchies, directed in their operations mainly by clear-sighted business men, using the political machinery of their country for the furtherance of their private interests. This by no means implies that states are equally aggressive, equally absolute and equally susceptible to business control. Still less does it imply that in the immediate causa-

tion of the war conscious economic conflicts of interests were
the efficient causes, or that direct causal responsibility is to be
distributed equally among the belligerent groups.   Indeed, the
account of nineteenth-century movements here presented, if
correct, explains why the German State became more absolu-
tist in its claims and powers than other states, more consciously
aggressive in its external policy and in recent years more definitely occupied with economic considerations.   Its geographical position, its meagre access to the sea, its rapid recent
career of industrialism, its growing need of foreign markets
and its late entrance upon the struggle for empire, all contrib-
uted to sharpen the sense of antagonism in German statecraft
and to make it more aggressive.   The pressures for forcible
expansion were necessarily stronger in this pent-up nation than
in those which enjoyed in a literal sense " the freedom of the
seas " and large dependencies for occupation, government, trade
priority and capitalistic exploitation.   The ruthless realism of
German statecraft, its habitual and successful reliance upon
military force, the tough strain of feudal tyranny and servitude,
surviving in the spirit of Prussian institutions, served to make
Germany in a quite peculiar degree the center of discord alike
in its internal and its external polity.   In the nation where
Marx and Bismarck had stamped their teaching so forcibly
upon the general mind, no great faith in the economic harmonies and pacific internationalism could be expected to survive.
To these distinctively realistic forces must be added the subtler
but not less significant contributions of Hegel and Darwin,
working along widely different channels to give a " scientific "
support to political autocracy, economic domination and an ab-
solutist state striving to enforce its will in a world of rival states
contending for survival and supremacy.   Out of that devil's
brew were concocted the heady doctrines of Treitschke and his
school, to whose educative influences such extravagant importance is attached by those who seek to represent the whole German nation as privy to a long-preconcerted plan for war.   That
large romantic theories, claiming scientific or philosophical
authority, have had, especially in Germany, a considerable influence in disposing the educated members of the ruling and

possessing classes to accept policies of force in the internal and external acts of government that seemed favorable to their interests and prestige, there can be no doubt. We know also that in Germany and elsewhere among the class-conscious leaders of socialist and labor movements a sort of semi-scientific sanction for the use of violence in a class war that was an inevitable phase in the evolution of a "new" society was based upon the same biological misconception.

But we must not be misled by ideologists or heated pamphleteers into imputing an excessive value to these theories regarded as actual forces in conduct. Were this value what it is pretended in some quarters, the war would not have come as a surprise. It would have been expected. The wide prevalence of doctrines of "force", rivalry of nations and struggle for survival on a basis of social efficiency, were not in any real sense determinant factors in bringing about the war. Nor did they do more than mitigate in more reflecting minds the profound astonishment which accompanied the outbreak of war. The really operative causes were the deep antagonism of interest and feeling which this analysis has disclosed or, conversely, the feebleness of the safeguards against war upon which liberal and humane thinkers had relied, *viz.*, economic internationalism, democracy and the restricted functions of the state.

J. A. HOBSON.

LONDON.

Article 11

This extract from Chapter IV of *Democracy after the War* is preceded by a discussion of the rise of Protectionism and the business interests which support it (pp. 68-77).

II

But the fuller nature of this conspiracy of vested interests against the Commonwealth is seen in the economic interpretation of Imperialism. Just as Protection originates in the desire of certain strong capitalistic industries to increase their private profits at the expense of the community by securing a monopoly of the home markets, so Imperialism originates in a desire of the same business interests to extend their gains by bringing under their national flag new territorial areas for profitable commerce and investment. They are under a powerful economic pressure to fasten on their Government this pushful foreign policy. For the large profits and high incomes drawn by the capitalistic and organizing classes in the great staple branches of industry and commerce involve a restriction of the home market and a consequent inability to find profitable employment for their large accumulations of savings. Where the product of industry and commerce is so divided that wages are low while profits, interest, rent are relatively high, the small purchasing power of the masses sets a limit on the home market for most staple commodities. For a comparatively small proportion of the well-to-do incomes, into which profits, interests, rents enter, is expended in demand for such commodities. The staple manufactures therefore, working with modern mechanical methods that continually increase the pace of output, are in every country compelled to look more and more to export trade, and to hustle and compete for markets in the backward countries of the world. So long as Britain was the workshop of the world, the full significance of this commercial competition did not appear. The world-market seemed to the Lancashire and Birmingham exporters of the early nineteenth century illimitable. But the last quarter of the century marked a rapid change. New nations had entered the career of industrial and commercial capitalism, and were invading the export markets of which we held possession, and were opening up or competing with one another for new markets. In each nation the home market had been found inadequate to take off the growing output, so that foreign outlets must be found or forced. Now, there is nothing in the general theory of trade to explain the situation which then emerged. Since all commerce is eventually exchange of goods against goods, markets ought to be illimitable as the wants of man. But just as the manufacturers and traders of each nation found their home markets limited, so they found the world-market also limited in the rate and pace of its expansion. In other words, the maximum output of the mines, mills and workshops in Britain, Germany, Belgium, France, the United States, etc., appeared to exceed not merely the demand of the home markets, but of the immediately available and profitable world-market. Nor is it really surprising that this should be so. For just as the home market was restricted by a distribution of wealth which left the mass of the people with inadequate power to purchase and consume, while the minority who had the purchasing power either wanted to use it in other ways, or to save it and apply it to an increased production which still further congested the home markets, so likewise with the world-market. The profits of the foreign trade and of the foreign industries which it sustained were distributed so unequally, and the gains to the masses of the peoples in the newly developed countries were relatively so small, that the same incapacity to purchase for consumption the whole volume of exported goods competing for sale was exhibited.

Closely linked with this practical limitation of the expansion of markets for goods is the limitation of profitable fields of investment. The limitation of home markets implies a corresponding limitation in the investment of fresh capital in the trades supplying these markets. This limitation of investment is not wholly removed if, as we see, the expansion of foreign markets for the same trade is also limited. So it is reasonable to expect that the demand for new capital for investment at home will absorb a smaller and smaller proportion of the whole volume of new capital which the wealthy saving classes will bring into existence. Putting the case concretely, only a limited proportion of the savings made by the capitalists in the textile trades of this country can be profitably absorbed in normal times in putting up more textile plant, either for supplying the home market or for world trade. And what is true of textiles will be true of a large proportion of the savings made from trade and industry. An increasing proportion of such savings must seek other investments. Now, it is not necessary here to discuss the delicate economic issue, whether it can rightly be maintained that there is any rigid limit to the quantity of new capital which can be absorbed in a modern country with all sorts of growing and potential wants and with indefinitely large improvements in the structure of industry. It is sufficient for our argument to affirm that, in fact, a growing tendency for new capital to seek and find more lucrative employment overseas has been exhibited. The financial and investing classes of every developed industrial nation have within the last generation been sending an increasing proportion of their ever-growing savings into backward countries. Now, though the work remaining to be done by capital in developing the resources of the world is practically infinite, at any given time the quantity of reasonably safe and profitable openings is limited. Thus there emerges the same pressure upon available opportunities for foreign investment that appears in the case of foreign markets. The supply of competing capital from different investing countries shows the same tendency to exceed the effective demand as in the case of ordinary foreign trade.

Indeed, so far as appearances go, there is nothing to distinguish the investment of capital abroad from ordinary export trade. For every loan, whether to a foreign monarch for his private extravagances, to a Government to enable it to buy warships or to make harbours, to a syndicate for railroad purposes, or to an industrial company in order to set up steel mills or textile factories, must take the form of an order for goods of some sort which are at the disposal of the investor, and which ordinarily consist of goods made in the country where the investor lives and does his business. If English investors find money for a new railway in the Argentine or Brazil, that investment acts as a demand for English goods which, as they pass out of this country, rank as so much

6

export trade. This is quite obvious when, as is common in French and German foreign contracts, it is made a condition that the foreign railway, or other company, shall take out the whole or a large part of the loan in French or German rails, engines or other stores. But, though less obvious, it is equally true when no such condition is made. If the money which English investors supply to an Argentine railway is directly expended in purchasing American rails and engines, the monetary operation compels the Americans or some other foreigners to buy English goods which otherwise they would not have bought. In other words, an investment of English capital abroad is in substance nothing else than an order for English goods, which must go out either to the borrowing country, or to some other with which it has commercial dealings, in fulfilment of the order. But the identity between export trade and foreign investment in the first instance does not affect the important distinction between the two processes in their subsequent career. The interest of the ordinary exporter in the country where he finds a market for his goods is limited to the consideration of the immediate gain he makes upon the goods he has sold and the hopes of further gains from future sales. This foreign market means something to him, and the good government and prosperity of the people in the foreign country are of some concern to him. If any serious trouble arises in the country which threatens to destroy his profitable market, or if some other Government tries to bring pressure to get away his market for their traders, he will try to get his Government to protect his interests. So the interests of groups of traders have played a considerable and a growing part in foreign policy, and the desire to acquire, preserve and improve foreign markets, especially in backward and ill-governed countries, has been a distinct and powerful motive in Imperialism. But after all, the stake which traders have in a foreign market is not nearly so great as that of investors. If traders fail to sell their wares in one market they can sell them, though perhaps less advantageously, in another. It is different for those who have invested their capital in a foreign country. They are in effect the owners of a portion of that country, they have a lien upon its railways, its land, plant, buildings, mines or other immovable property. Their stake is a fixed and lasting one, it is bound up with the general prosperity or failure of the country. Their economic interest in that foreign country may be as great as or greater than in their own, and what happens for good or evil in that country may be more important to them than anything likely to happen in their own. If, therefore, any action of their Government, any stroke of foreign policy, can improve the security of that distant country, it improves their securities, and even if a threat of war or an act of war is needed to obtain that object, what matter? The people pay the cost with their lives and their money, the investor and the financier reap the gain. What was said by a British statesman in a moment of illumination in the early stage of our absorption of Egypt, "The trail of finance is over it all," is applicable to most modern instances of Imperialism. Not only is the stake of the financier and the investor greater than that of the mere trader, but his power to influence the foreign policy of his Government is usually stronger. It is more concentrated, wielded more skilfully, and is more direct in its action.

The enormous recent growth of foreign investments among the well-to-do means that when any foreign country comes into the purview of our national policy, there are men in our governing classes whose personal fortunes are affected for good or evil by its handling. This dominating and directing influence of investments in our imperial and foreign policy is well illustrated in the events culminating in the Boer War and the annexation of the two Dutch Republics. I know no instance in which the dominant drive of economic interests was more manifest. The powerful desire and intention of the vigorous and pushful business men upon the Rand, to strengthen their hold upon the gold reef so as to secure for themselves its profitable output and to escape the taxation, blackmailing and other obstructive duties of a foolish and incompetent Government, were beyond all question the determinant forces in the policy that was formulated. This statement, however, must be harmonized with the equally true statement that neither the British people, nor the British Government, nor the vast majority of British South Africans were motived mainly, or at all consciously, by any such economic motive. The chief agents of this policy, Chamberlain, Rhodes and Lord Milner, were, so far as history shows, actuated by political motives in which the idea of imperial expansion doubtless coalesced with the sense of personal ambition, but in which distinctively economic gains either for themselves or for others played no determinant part. In the case of Chamberlain and Lord Milner the absence of economic motive is indisputable. They worked to precipitate a struggle which should bring the downfall and the annexation of the Dutch Republics, because they wished to secure a federation of South African States under the British Flag as a step desirable in itself and still more as a contribution towards the larger ideal of Imperial Federation which Chamberlain had espoused as the goal of his colonial policy. The case of Rhodes was different. His economic interests were identified with those of the other business men upon the Rand, and the subtle bonds between property and personal power must be held to have exercised a powerful influence upon his policy. But even here there is no reason to doubt the genuineness of his passion for imperial expansion as a desirable end, or the enthusiasm expressed in his phrase " The North is my idea."

The great volume of feeling, both in South Africa and in this country, which favoured forcible interference with the two Republics, was almost wholly free from conscious economic bias. The demand for the franchise and the whole tale of Outlanders' grievances were based upon political and humanitarian sentiment. The alleged maltreatment of British subjects was fortified by the barbarity of the native policy in the Republics and driven home by the fable of the great Boer conspiracy to " drive the British into the sea." Justice, humanity, prestige, expansion, political ambition, all conspired to dwarf the significance of the business motive. But persistence, point, direction and intelligible aim belonged to the latter. The financiers of De Beers, the Rand

and the Chartered Company, are, therefore, rightly recognized as " engineering " the policy which brought war and conquest. No doubt they could not have succeeded in getting what they wanted, viz. improved security for present and prospective investments, had it not been for the personal ambition of a British statesman and the political and humanitarian sentiments behind him. But these non-economic motives were a fund of loose, ill-directed force for them to utilize. Nor were the methods of doing this obscure. They needed to control the British Press and politics of South Africa. It was not difficult for the owners or managers of the sole sources of wealth in such a country to compass this. They owned the Press and they were the politicians. From South Africa they operated upon public opinion in Great Britain. Society and its political support was purchased by directorates and well-planted blocks of shares. When the appointed time came to force upon public opinion and national policy the mine-owners' policy, agents of the Rand financiers " saw " the politicians and editors of both parties, organized a missionary campaign among the Churches to expose the cruel treatment of the Kaffirs, and through their command of the cables and the Press of South Africa poured " Outlander atrocities " and " Dutch conspiracy " into the innocent mind of the British public. When the issue of war was trembling in the balance, the widespread ownership of mining shares in hundreds of influential local circles all over the country secretly assisted to mobilize public opinion in favour of determined action. Though the diplomacy which precipitated war was conducted by politicians, the policy it developed and enforced was designed, directed, and prepared in detail by business men in South Africa and London. While the Prime Minister declared quite veraciously, so far as he and the bulk of the British nation were concerned, "We seek no gold fields, we seek no territory," the war policy was imposed on him by those who sought those very objects.

This classic modern instance of Imperialism presents in clearest outline the relation between economic and non-economic factors in foreign policy. It was only exceptional in the directly conscious nature of its "engineering." In most instances the cloak of patriotism is worn more skilfully, and the blend of business interests with racial or nationalist sentiment, with historic memories and claims, with considerations of frontier defence, balance of power, and the fears, suspicions and enmities that relate thereto, is more baffling to analyse.

Moreover, foreign policy and the relation between States involved therein must not be envisaged merely in terms of opposition and of conflict. There is in the modern widening of human intercourse a large and various growth of common interests and activities among men of different nations which for certain purposes requires and evokes the friendly co-operation of States and calls into being genuinely international institutions. Much of the inter-State apparatus of intercourse, of which the Inter-postal Union may be cited as a leading instance, is so manifestly beneficial to all parties that any slight differences of interest which may arise in ordinary times are easily adjusted. So obviously serviceable is this network of peaceful

co-operation between members of different political
communities that it has operated to cloak the real
dangers of the situation. Economic cosmopolitanism
in trade and finance, with the inter-State arrangements
to which I have referred, has appeared to give such
powerful and such growing guarantees of peace
that pacifists have been accustomed to denounce
as obsolete mediævalism the statecraft which eyes
other States with enmity or with suspicion, and
which seeks national security in armed preparations.
This pacifist illusion was based upon a belief that in
modern civilized States the art of government was so
conducted in really critical issues as to express the
will and serve the interests of the peoples. It ought
not, however, to have needed this war to dispel
that illusion. Neither the economic nor the human
solidarity of interests between men of different nations
avails to keep the peace, if powerful business groups
within these nations, with a grasp upon their governmental policy, find their interests in collision. We
have already seen how modern capitalism has gener-
ated these group antagonisms of business interests
in modern industrial nations, driving them to force
on their respective Governments related policies of
Protectionism and Imperialism which require the
permanent support of militarism and navalism and
the occasional recourse to war. The cosmopolitanism which is a growing characteristic of the modern
business world is crossed and reversed by business
antagonisms masquerading as " national " whenever
these group forces find it profitable to control and
use their respective Governments. The competing
Imperialism of the last forty years has been quite

manifestly directed by this *motif*. It has been a struggle for markets, loans, concessions, and opportunities for profitable exploitation in weak or backward countries, in which the Governments of the Great Powers have schemed and fought in connivance with or at the behest of strong business organizations. We have cited the instance of the Transvaal. But a brief general survey of the chief danger-areas in recent world-politics is required to drive the lesson home.

What are these areas of international disturbances and imperialist ambitions ? Egypt, Congo, Morocco, Transvaal, Persia, Tripoli, China, Mexico, Anatolia and Mesopotamia, the Balkans. With wide variety of circumstances, the essential story is the same. Trading and financial interests play upon political fears and desires, in order to gain their profitable ends. Where finance wins predominance as the economic motive, this manipulation of political motives and actions becomes more and more the clue to international entanglements. It is true that in some instances political motives have an independent origin. Where it happens that in the co-operation of " imperialist " policy and economic exploitation each " uses " the other, the financier recognizes the advantages of keeping in the background. This was even the case in Egypt. Though Lord Cromer's opening sentence in his " Modern Egypt " announces that " The origin of the Egyptian question in its modern phase was financial," and the story of the English and French creditors pressing their Governments to foreclose upon the property has been attested by convincing testimony, most Britons prefer to accept the purely political interpretation of the episode. Even Mr. Hartley Withers, ignoring the actual evidence of the financial pressure on the Ministry, and the doctrine of the obligation of the Government to safeguard the life and property of British subjects in foreign parts, established by the famous instance of Don Pacifico, assigns the efficient causation to diplomacy, not to finance. Now, it is true, as he urges,[1] that the position of Egypt on the route to India made it appear important to our statesmen that our Government should have a hold upon the country. But when Mr. Withers suggests that, alike in purchasing shares in the Suez Canal and in using the claims of English bondholders as an excuse for establishing its power in Egypt, English diplomacy was using finance, instead of being used by it, he ignores the plain fact that the political motive in each instance lay idle until it was stimulated into activity by the more energetic and constructive policy of the financier.

It is doubtless true that finance is not equally capable of utilizing diplomacy under all circumstances. " If Egypt had been Brazil," says Mr. Withers, " it is not very likely that the British Fleet would have shelled Rio de Janeiro." But this instance, cited to show that the motive force in the Egyptian episode was not financial, shows the opposite. For it provides the " exception " that " proves the rule." The reason why Rio de Janeiro would not have been shelled is found in the Monroe Doctrine and the strength of the United States. In other words, the financial game of politics can only be played out in ill-defended

[1] " International Finance," pp. 98-102.

countries. A recent American writer has well-expressed the economic and political conditions which conspire to make a country a bone of political contention :—

It is essential to remember that what turns a territory into a diplomatic problem is the combination of natural resources, cheap labour markets, defencelessness, corrupt and inefficient government.[1]

Apply these conditions to each of the above-named areas of trouble, and you will find that they fit the situation. Financial and commercial policy take different shapes in different cases.

Sometimes the initial wedge of financial interest consists in feeding the extravagances of a spendthrift monarch, as in Egypt and Morocco, or in pressing loans upon a backward country for undefined work of " development," which often includes expenditure on armaments. Such have been the early dealings with Turkey and with certain South American States. But generally there has existed, even at the outset, a more concrete business object, the development of railroads or of mining resources, the working of rubber plantations, oil wells, or some other rich, natural source of wealth. When mere trade has given an initial impulse, the organization of labour within the country, for working and collecting and marketing the trade-objects, ivory, rubber, etc., has soon taken command of the situation, as on the Amazon, in Congo, and in Angola. So practical Imperialism has commonly worked out in a system of servile and

[1] Mr. Walter Lippman, "The Stakes of Diplomacy," p. 93.

forced labour imposed by white superintendents for the advantage of financiers and shareholders in London, Paris, Berlin or Brussels. Although political ambitions and rivalries figure most prominently, the real contentions have usually been between two or more groups of business men in different nations, pulling diplomatic strings in favour of the special concessions which they seek in one of these undeveloped areas. As more Western nations have felt the need for outside markets in which to buy and sell and to invest their surplus wealth, these financial pressures upon foreign policy have been more urgent and the controversies which they have stirred up more acute. While foreign and colonial ministers have been in the habit of parading political exigencies and patriotic sentiments in favour of their special foreign policy, the patient forces in the background, moulding that policy, become in every decade more definitely financial. Now, if, as is sometimes pretended, the finance were genuinely international or cosmopolitan, instead of exciting it might allay the friction between Governments. There have been moments and occasions when the financial arrangements between business groups in different countries have been a pacific force. This was the case at one time in regard to Morocco, when a combine of the Mannesmann and Creusot interests for the common exploitation of the iron ore of that country seemed on the point of bringing the German and French Governments into a harmonious arrangement. A similar harmony between opposed financial interests of traders and bankers was brought about in Persia when the British and Russian Governments divided up the country into separate spheres of exploitation. But of course there are two defects in such economic settlements, regarded from the standpoint of political adjustment. They have commonly 'been confined to two or three national interests and have frozen out the trading or financial interests of some other Powers, as was the case with German interests in Persia. Moreover, these arrangements, forced upon the Government and people of the backward State, have little permanence or security, and are likely to lead to further intrigues on the part of the " vulture " Governments, each hungry for a larger share of the prey, and likely to endeavour to stir up internal disturbances as a means of finding satisfaction for its ever-growing appetite.

The story of the various measures taken by financial groups in various countries, with the active support of their respective Foreign Offices, to promote the financial penetration of China, is the crucial example of the interplay of foreign policy and finance. The full history of the fluctuating policy of the Powers in their treatment of China, now moving towards partition into separate spheres of influence and exploitation, now reverting to " the open door," the changing combinations of Government-assisted groups in the leading countries, and the attempt of outside financial adventurers to break the ring, will perhaps never emerge from its underground passages into the clear light of day. But enough has come out in official documents, Parliament and the Press, to enable us to construct with a fair amount of certitude the main instructive outlines of the episode.

In China, as elsewhere, war sowed the seeds of a

monetary embarrassment, of which money-lenders were to reap a rich harvest. In 1894 China, in difficulties to find the war-indemnity imposed by Japan, was driven to negotiate a 7 per cent. loan through the Hong-Kong and Shanghai Bank. Next year a combination of two French banks issued a China loan. In 1896 an alliance between the Hong-Kong and the Deutsch-Asiatisch Bank, which lasted through the next sixteen years, laid a solid basis of international political pressure, leading to the floating of a number of Chinese Government loans, on highly profitable terms to British and German financiers. The suppression of the Boxer trouble in 1899 by the joint forces of the Powers had two consequences. First, it left a large new indemnity, a fresh source of political-financial pressure for the several Powers. Secondly, it dissipated for some time the " partition " policy, which had revived with the territorial aggressions of Germany, Russia and Japan, and led, under the active pressure of America, to the formal adoption of " the open door " for commerce and financial enterprise. The British-German " consortium " held the field until 1911, when, largely as a result of diplomatic pressure, French and American banking groups were brought into the alliance, known henceforth as the Four-Power Group. The inclusion of America, not at that time a lending country and therefore suspected of political aims, brought about next year such pressure from the Russian and the Japanese Governments that it was necessary to admit their nominees, the Russo-Asiatic Bank and the Yokohama Specie Bank, into the arrangement, henceforth designated the Six-Power Group. Regarded as a financial arrangement, the addition of Russia and Japan brought no new strength. For, if they were to lend money, they must first borrow it, swelling the costs with the profits of unnecessary middlemen, and utilizing this finance quite evidently for political purposes.

The motives of the Governments which promoted these financial arrangements were doubtless mixed. Two of them, Russia and Japan, were actuated primarily by considerations of territorial and political aggrandisement. The Governments of these countries expressly demanded that their " rights and special interests," i.e. in Manchuria, Mongolia, etc., should be recognized, and Germany, recently planted in Kiaochow, was doubtless animated by a desire to fasten a political as well as an industrial control over the province of Shantung. Great Britain, France, and America stood in the main for the territorial integrity and political independence of China and for an "open door." But even this statement requires qualification. For France more than once was pulled by her Russian alliance into favouring the assertion of special Russian interests in Mongolia, while Great Britain still retained some sort of special lien upon the exploitation of the Yang Tse Valley.

In the various pressures exerted by the Two, Four and Six-Power Groups upon the Chinese Government to borrow money in constantly increasing quantities, it is not possible to prove how far the initiative was taken by the financial groups, how far by the Foreign Offices. No doubt it seemed diplomatically desirable to entangle a Government like that of China with burdens of indebtedness which might at any time be

utilized for political ends. But with the exception
of the two Eastern Powers, the main drive of interests
was admittedly economic, not political, and the foreign
policy of their Governments must be regarded as
having been moved and directed primarily by finance.
This judgment is powerfully corroborated by the
extraordinary attitude taken by our Foreign Office
upon the two occasions when other financial groups
sought to enter the field and to furnish China with
the money she required, upon terms which seemed
desirable to the Chinese Government. The first case
was that of an international syndicate of Russian,
French, Belgian and English groups, of which the
leading English body was the Eastern Bank, which
endeavoured in 1912, unsuccessfully, to obtain the
Foreign Office sanction for participating in any
future loans arranged with the Chinese Government.
The reasons given for the refusal by the Foreign
Office deserve to be placed on record.

In regard to loans in China, it is impossible for the
moment for His Majesty's Government to support negotiations for a loan which might conflict with the terms or
weaken the security for the large loan for reorganiza-
tion purposes which is at present being negotiated in
Pekin by the Four-Power combine, with the full knowledge
of their respective Governments, and in regard to which
advances have already been made to the Chinese Government by the banks interested, with the full approval of
their Governments. I am to add that, as a matter of
principle, His Majesty's Government would not feel
justified in giving their support to any loan which did
not, in their opinion, and in the opinion of the other
Governments concerned, offer adequate guarantees for

the proper and useful expenditure of the proceeds and satisfactory security for the payment of principal and interest.

Here, then, we have the admission of a private profiteering scheme of financiers of different countries, described as " a Four-Power combine," authorized and supported by their respective Governments, which undertake to secure for them a monopoly in loanmongering by refusing the assistance which any other group would require in dealing with a foreign Government. Not merely do the Governments refuse "support" to competing financiers who are offering money to China upon better terms than the authorized groups; they actually oppose and obstruct such healthy competition. Of this we may cite two illustrations. The first is the stoppage of a loan of two millions arranged by a Belgian syndicate for the construction of a Chinese railway. This was stopped by the veto of the French Government upon a quotation on the Bourse, the explanation being " French obligations to the other five Powers." In other words, Belgium was outside the Government authorized ring. The second more famous example was the treatment by our Foreign Office of the Crisp loan, a loan of ten millions organized in London by a powerful syndicate of banks. When Mr. Crisp, disregarding the representations of our Foreign Office to the effect that " His Majesty's Government did not consider that China was free to borrow outside the consortium until the repayment of the advances made by the latter had been duly provided for," proceeded to carry his arrangements to a con-

7

clusion, Sir Edward Grey telegraphed to our Pekin
Minister :—

I am in communication with them (the Crisp Syndicate)
with the view to stopping the execution of the agreement,
if possible. Should I fail in that, it will become necessary
to deal with the matter by direct communication with the
Chinese Government.

Mr. Gregory, of the Foreign Office, informed Mr.
Crisp that " they could put considerable pressure on
the Chinese Government, and would not hesitate to
do so at once."   A little later on we find our Foreign
Office telegraphing to our Pekin Minister that if the
Chinese Government does sanction the Crisp loan
" His Majesty's Government will be obliged to take
the most serious view of such proceedings."

You are aware that we are disposed to show every
consideration to the Chinese Government in facilitating
their negotiations with the groups, but our attitude will
have to be entirely reconsidered if the Chinese Government on their part defy us in a matter in which they know
that we are pledged to act with the five other Powers.

But in considering this curious conspiracy between
financial groups and Governments, it is well to draw
attention to the concluding sentence in Sir Edward
Grey's despatch, as quoted above.   For it asserts the
extraordinary doctrine that when private financiers
arrange a loan with a foreign Government, the State
of which these financiers are nationals not merely
shall see that the guarantees for repayment are
adequate but shall supervise the expenditure of the

money that is advanced. In other words, Stock Exchange financiers are not to be considered fit persons to take care of their own interests abroad, and foreign Governments are not fit to decide how the money which they borrow may be used. It is very difficult to understand how far this interfering policy is actuated by political and how far by financial considerations. On the evidence, it seems as if groups of financiers had leagued together to induce their Governments to bring united pressure on the Chinese Government to borrow larger sums of money than were wanted, and to admit into this financial participation Powers which, like Russia and Japan, had no money of their own to lend but had heavy political axes to grind. Although the Foreign Offices of European Powers may have been actuated in part by the principle that it was best to act in concert so as to prevent loans from individual groups which would be used to obtain political advantages for particular countries as against the general advantage of China itself, it is practically certain that business men ran this policy for all it was worth, seeing how it might be worked to secure for them a " cinch " upon this profitable lending. They were to find the money, their Government was to extort guarantees for the security of this money and, by stopping the competition of other groups, either in their own country or elsewhere, to secure for them better terms than they could have got had the business been conducted on the principle of " the open door." *The Times*, in writing of the incident, described the Six-Power Group as the " financial agents " of their Governments. But it would probably be more

consonant with the facts to describe the Government
as the " political agents " of the groups. One thing
is tolerably clear, viz. that " the general advantage
of China " played no real part in determining the
action either of groups or Governments.

The financiers were after safe and profitable loans,
the Governments were either after spheres of influence,
as with Russia and Japan, or after preventing one
another from pursuing a separate and exclusive
policy of marking out areas of political and economic
control.

This joint political-financial coercion of China
eventually broke down.   But as an episode in foreign
policy it is most illuminating.   For it shows from a
typical modern instance how the money power within
each State is able to utilize a foreign policy, in which
Governments are continually wobbling between conflicting " principles " of " spheres of influence " and
" open door," for the purpose of promoting lucrative
financial operations.   For the business men of the
Great Powers, China is a huge field of commercial and
financial exploitation, and their respective Governments with their shifty policies are tools for its profitable working.   During the war Japan and Russia
have utilized the great advantage of proximity, and
when the fog is once more cleared will be found to
have played havoc with the " open door," forcing
their exclusive pretensions, commercial and political,
upon large areas which they had already marked
down for absorption.

Such has been the common history of the processes
by which countries, which had begun by being
" areas of legitimate aspiration " to powerful business

groups, pass along the diplomatically graded path towards "spheres of influence," protectorates or colonial possessions. No doubt it is true that when this takes place politics is " in it " on its own account, as well as business, but the active initiation and direction are generally exercised by the latter. Even in those modern instances of French and Russian Imperialism, where political pride or distinctively territorial ambitions figure most prominently, the " dark forces " of finance have been constantly operative in the background.

Once more I repeat, it is not a question of the volume of power but of its direction. Political and sentimental policy is more fluctuating and volatile than economic policy. The late Sir James Stephen truly said, " The world is made for hard practical men who know what they want and mean to get it." Though " practical " is not wholly synonymous with " business," the business world furnishes by far the largest scope for " hard practical " ability. Imperialism is the decorative title for the widest operation of this practical ability, and militarism and navalism are essential instruments for its profitable exercise.

Article 12

ECONOMIC INTERNATIONALISM

§ As we have stated these principles of income and its uses, they are fully applicable only to a completely self-contained economic system, i.e. to the whole world of effective economic intercourse, or to some virtually self-contained nation. When we seek to apply them to nations whose members are in close marketing relations with the members of other nations, or where considerable freedom of migration exists, modifications and retardations in the application of these principles are inevitable. An illustration is furnished by the contrast between the present condition of employment in France and in Britain. France, still a semi-industrialised country, with less inequality of incomes than Britain, a rigorously controlled growth of population, and an obstructive tariff system which makes her less dependent than most other advanced countries upon economic intercourse with outside areas, has virtually no unemployed capital and labour. Britain, more fully industrialised, dependent upon outside markets for essential foods and many raw materials, and for the disposal of her growing output of manufactures, and with a still growing population, is confronted with an apparently insoluble problem of unemployment.

If there were free trade, free mobility of capital and labour, throughout the economic world, with more effective international banking and finance, it seems to some economists that full employment, maximum productivity, and such a distribution of the 'surplus' as would satisfy all reasonable claims of equity and humanity would ensue. But to the attainment of any such ideals there are two related obstacles. The first is an uncontrolled industrialism under new conditions of technique and organisation spreading rapidly through hitherto backward and undeveloped countries. The second is a continuing rapid increase of world population, of which a growing proportion consists of coloured peoples adaptable to labour under white control and at low rates of real wages.

Now, here enters a new possibility of danger, which elsewhere I have designated Inter-imperialism, an economic international co-operation of advanced industrial peoples for the exploitation of the labour and the undeveloped natural resources of backward countries, chiefly in Africa and Asia. It would be feasible for the Capitalist groups in the advanced countries to suspend their costly struggles for areas of exploitation, conducted with the forced aid of their respective Governments, and accompanied, as a costly by-product, by great and little wars, and to work in friendly co-operation for the common exploitation of these backward countries and their peoples. Such an international economic policy easily emerges from a growth of international Cartels in many fields. Oil, copper, rubber, cotton, and a growing number of raw materials point to the progress of such international operations, conducted with the connivance or active support of the several Governments whose group-interests are involved.

There is a growing disposition to move in this direction on the part of Big Business threatened by the growing Trade Unionism and political power of white workers. Why should not labour troubles caused by white workers and their socialistic legislation be bought off by high wages and other good conditions at the expense of the backward peoples? Thus the economic division of interests might take a new shape. For the cleavage between Capital and Labour, or strong and weak industries, in the Western World might be substituted a less dangerous division. But, regarding the economic system as a whole, this policy could only hope to ease the immediate situation in the West. It could offer no final remedy to the disease of an inadequate expansion of markets due to maldistribution of purchasing power. It could only alter the shape of the problem. A world-commerce system conducted under such conditions would retain and very probably enhance the inequality of income which, as we have seen, disables effective demand for commodities from keeping pace with the increase of the industrial producing power. Nothing short of a continuous advance in the consuming power of the great, new backward peoples with their increasing numbers could find adequate employment for the constant advances of productive power in the countries equipped with modern methods of manufacture.

§ But since neither in a competitive industrial system nor in the new cartelised system which presses to take its place is there any reasonable hope of developing a price and wage system which shall stimulate adequately this advance of effective demand in backward countries, we appear to be faced with a continual recurrence of cycles of grave depression in the manufacturing industries of the advanced countries, and their familiar reactions upon finance, commerce, and agriculture. It is these experiences, and fears of their repetition, that drive most industrial nations into protection in a vain effort to retain a home market adequate to the demands of the new productive technique. The effort must be vain, for even if this protective system brought a rising standard of wages for a controlled population, that rising standard could not keep pace with the growing productivity of manufactures. An industrial country cannot in the long run live on its home market. It must continually seek more foreign areas in which to buy and sell and invest and develop.

Some alleviation of this situation is, however, possible. So far as a greater equalisation of income in an industrialised country is attainable, either by Trade Union organisation (with restriction on the growth of workers' families), or by political action in the shape of minimum wages and maximum hours regulations, or by public subsidies levied upon surplus income, the otherwise wasteful elements of surplus can be converted into human welfare. So far as this equalisation of income stimulates consumption, and reduces the proportion of attempted material 'saving', it will furnish larger employment for industrial resources, employing more of the new saving at home and exporting less of it. This more equal distribution of income would thus reduce the proportion of income saved, though not necessarily the amount of saving. For the total product and income would be larger. It would tend to restrict the pace of growth of industrial capital by diverting much of the potential new industrial capital to direct human consumption, either as personal income or as social welfare. This policy would bring a fuller use of productive resources, greater total productivity, and greater human benefit from the larger aggregate income, or from its substitute, the larger leisure.

But though a single nation, like Britain, might put into operation this improved economy with some benefit, it could not get or retain the full human or economic gain, unless some corresponding movement towards equalisation of incomes and enlargement of consuming powers was taking place in all or most other countries forming integral parts of the world-economic system. For if in a single country, e.g. Britain, this policy were in operation, new capital would tend to flow into other countries where a sweating economy was still feasible. Penalties or prohibitions upon such enlarged export of capital, if effective, would make for an isolated economic state which, in the case of Britain, might bring such impoverishment that a better distribution of the reduced product would not yield a net gain of welfare.

So far as free mobility of flow of capital and goods exists, it is impossible to guarantee full employment in a single country. If labour were as mobile as capital, actual unemployment might not occur. What would happen would be that less productive work was done in some national areas, more in others, for the benefit of the world-economic system. But labour continues to be far less mobile than capital. This is partly because labour consists of labourers, human beings with attachments and interests outside the economic sphere, who are not willing to place themselves indifferently in any part of the world where higher wages call them. Still more potent are the obstacles put upon free immigration in countries where organised labour can conserve its superior economic status by legal restrictions upon entrance into its sphere.

§ These considerations make it evident that full productivity and employment can only be attainable in such a country as Britain by a combination of two lines of economic policy. An internal policy of higher wages and of taxation directed to secure for public expenditure a larger share of rents and other surplus incomes would, by increasing the current consumption or demand for commodities, at once permit fuller employment of all existing productive resources, and stimulate employers and their brain-workers to discover and apply the best methods of technique and organisation. It is possible that this policy, boldly pursued, might so reduce costs of production per unit of the product in industry and agriculture as might not only hold the home market against foreign competition in manufactured goods, but also secure so large an export market as to pay for all the larger importations of food and raw materials which the enlarged consumption of our population would require. On this hypothesis we could, out of the better use of our own hands and brains, by a policy of better internal distribution, so raise our productivity as to secure economic health and progress without external assistance. But this assumes that other industrial nations are not cutting their costs of production by operating the new technique without any corresponding measures for the better and more equal distribution of consuming power. A policy of low wages, long hours, and low taxation in other industrial countries competing with us in the world-market might still enable them to secure so large a share of the limited[1] world-market as to continue to restrict the output of our export trades.

§ It is essential that Labour in this country should recognise the limitations of a High-Wage Short-Hours policy for our workers. In every industry there are obvious limits to 'the economy of high wages' in the promotion of efficiency. Though it is true that in America high wages, established during times when there was a relative shortage of hired labour, have been both cause and effect of efficient machine production, in Germany and other Continental countries high technical equipment is operated on a definitely lower wage and hours standard. Our recent losses of important foreign markets are

[1] i.e. limited by the failure of world-markets to keep pace with the rising powers of world-production.

undoubtedly attributable in part to the lower costs of labour in nations competing for a limited world-market. Under such conditions it will not be possible for us to maintain a standard of living much higher than that of our trade competitors. This would be realised more clearly if the final irrelevance of political barriers to trade were not obscured by tariffs and other false pretences that nations are trading with one another. It is only individual businesses or individual men who conduct trade. Everybody is aware that, if some English firms in a competitive business can get cheaper labour than other English firms, it is an advantage to them in getting contracts within this country. It is just as certain that, if these English firms are competing with foreign firms for contracts, the lower labour-costs of the foreigners will help them to outbid our firms. When low wages are accompanied by inferior capital equipment, the lower wage-bill may be offset by the inferior plant. But where technique and organisation are combined with lower wage-rates, as in Germany, it is foolish to suppose that legal or Trade Union action can maintain wages in this country at a definitely higher level. They can do so in the sheltered trades but at the expense of the unsheltered, and with ever-growing difficulty in exporting goods enough to pay for the foreign goods and materials we require, and in taking our part in the development of backward countries. That this last function is far less important than before has already been admitted. Other nations, America in particular, can afford to export capital in larger quantities for world-development. Moreover, the approaching stabilisation of our population reduces the importance of providing increased funds of foreign food and materials.

Nevertheless, we cannot afford to shut our eyes to the fact that our world-trade supremacy has gone and is irrecoverable. Rationalisation may help us to recover some foreign markets, but not if it is accompanied by wage-standards that disregard those of well-equipped foreign competitors. If, as there is no doubt, large bodies of surplus profits, rents, and other un-earned incomes exist in this country, taxation is a better instrument for a social policy of utilising them than wage-raising. For wage-raising in a competitive trade destroys the weaker businesses, and enables the surviving stronger ones to raise the price of the product, either by combination or by the reduction of supply due to the elimination of the weaker businesses. A progressive profit-tax has no such effect, and simply diverts to public revenue and social services what the trade can afford to pay. The pressure for expansion in our foreign market more and more takes the shape of seeking trade in backward countries, and is a struggle for this trade with exporters from countries that were once our customers. That enormous potential markets exist in Africa, China, and elsewhere there can be no doubt, but the expansion of these markets requires a complete reversal of the economic exploitation that has hitherto prevailed in the relations between advanced and backward countries. So long as a large part of the food and raw materials raised in tropical and other backward, non-industrial countries is the product of ill-paid or servile labour, the low consumption of imported manufactures in these countries will serve as a real restraint upon the productivity and full employment of the manufacturing trades in the exporting nations. A policy of better distribution of income in this country requires, therefore, to be supported by a corresponding movement in other countries, both those in direct competition with us as exporters of manufactured goods and those which produce the foods and raw materials we require, and receive in payment our manufactures.

For Product Safety Concerns and Information please contact our EU
representative GPSR@taylorandfrancis.com Taylor & Francis Verlag GmbH,
Kaufingerstraße 24, 80331 München, Germany

Printed and bound by CPI Group (UK) Ltd, Croydon, CR0 4YY
01/05/2025
01858342-0004